Insights
Into
Excellence

Updated Edition 1989

RH COMMUNICATIONS, INC.
P.O. Box 271177
Escondido, CA 92027

Printed in the United States of America.
ISBN 0-929887-01-8

ACKNOWLEDGEMENTS

This book is dedicated to the more than 30,000 Corporate and Association Meeting Planners who have entrusted the 20 members of Speakers Associates to positively impact their people.

Special thanks go to Steve Williford and Britt Densford for their editorial assistance.

Insights Into Excellence

CONTENTS

1

FIVE KEYS TO
EXCELLENCE

Jim Newman
P.O. Box 1378
Studio City, CA 91604
818/769-5100

How do you feel about the idea that people have a lot of potential that they don't use? That's pretty easy to see, isn't it? Especially in other people!

For most of us it is not as comfortable to look at the areas in which we have untapped potential. Yet that is just as true for you and me as it is for the people with whom we live and work.

"I know how to do that! How come I blew it?"

You're not the only person who ever had that thought!

William James, the famous American psychologist and philosopher, said that he thought the average person uses about 10% of their potential. I think he was probably high in his estimate. Now you are probably not an "average" person. You probably use a lot more than 10% of your abilities and talents — but can you see that there is a gap between *potential* and *performance* in your life?

That may be difficult to confront, frustrating to think

about, but it is a giant first step to increased excellence and success. I'd like to explore some of the reasons people don't use all of the potential they have. Even more important, I'd like to tell you about five keys that can open the door to much greater success in every sector of your life.

Can you get excited about the idea of being the best you can be? Not necessarily being better, or more successful, than someone else — being better than you have ever been! What I am going to share with you is based on the idea that one of the most thrilling opportunities any of us has is the chance to become what we can be.

First, let's define some terms and take a look at a simple "model" of what makes people behave as we do.

I'm going to be using the word "potential" to mean the present time accumulation in your system of inborn talent, acquired knowledge and skills and whatever motivation you have to make productive use of those inborn and acquired abilities. I believe that everyone is born "motivated" to grow and become. When people do not act as though they are motivated it's because there's something else going on in the system that is squelching or limiting that natural, inborn desire to excel.

Well then, if everyone really does want to use their abilities, why doesn't it happen? Why does the salesperson sit and look at the telephone for 30 minutes and not pick it up to call a prospect? Why does a parent who really loves a child and wants the best for that young person explode, scream and perhaps even become physically violent? The answer to that may seem too simple, but it is just this: The human system is primarily an emotional system.

Oh, the intellect is terribly important to be sure. The knowledge that you have acquired through educational and training programs is vital to your success. But you can have a lot of knowledge and information about something and still perform very badly. Or sometimes a person has only a little bit of potential in a particular area and handles the situation very well. It turns out that how you feel about yourself, your job, your relationships and your future is even more important than what you know about them.

Positive emotions tend to enhance the flow of whatever potential a person has – negative emotions block that flow.

If you will identify some areas of your life that are really "working" it is almost a certainty that those will be areas in which you have some very positive feelings. Joy, enthusiasm, excitement, fulfillment are some examples. You may be tempted to think that you have positive emotions because that area of your life is on track and I am inviting you to look at the possibility that the reason those areas are working so well is because of the positive emotions!

The other side of the coin is even easier to observe. What was the negative emotion that kept the salesperson from lifting up the telephone? Sure! It was fear! Fear of failure, fear of rejection or maybe a combination of both! What was the emotion that caused the parent to explode and strike out? Anger, frustration?

Now all of those are "normal" human emotions. I am suggesting that to the degree that they build up in your system and virtually "take over" control of your behavior, you are likely to handle that situation less well than you are capable of handling it. Negative emotions block the flow of potential.

Have you ever driven a car with the brakes on?

Not too bright! Not good for the car – or for the miles per gallon! Yet most of us who drive very much have probably occasionally found ourselves driving with the hand-brake partly set. And if that has ever happened to you, see if you can recall how it felt when you reached down and released the brakes, a sort of surging, "that's more like it" feeling.

Of course, you could have just pressed harder on the accelerator! That would probably have made the car go a little faster, but it would have wasted a lot of energy. Better by far to release the brakes and allow the horsepower to get to the wheels!

Do you see the parallel? We all drive through life with our emotional brakes partly set! One solution is to grit your teeth, clench your fists and try hard to do things better. I'm sure that you have tried that system. The tragedy is that "will power" often has a backlash effect. It is actually hazardous to your health! What works better is to get acquainted with the braking mechanisms and then release those brakes to allow your potential to flow!

Let's look at some releasing mechanisms. I'd like to invite you to consider five specific positive attitudes which will enhance excellence in your life — at home and on the job. As you allow these patterns to develop in your thought/feeling system you will see some dramatic changes happening in your ability to achieve your goals quickly, easily and with a lot more joy in the journey!

One of the fascinating attitudes that seems to be a common denominator of high-performance people is a pattern I call "growth-orientation." People who excel are excited about learning, growing and becoming.

I recall a program that I conducted several years ago for a national meeting of the Young Presidents Organization. YPO is made up of young, dynamic, successful men and women and their conventions are called "Universities For Presidents." They do have some social activities, to be sure, but the primary purpose of their meetings is to provide the members with a unique opportunity to learn from expert "resources" who are brought in to share their ideas and experiences with the YPOers.

I was scheduled to conduct a class at 8:45 one morning. I went to the meeting room a little before 8:00 to be sure everything was properly set up and was surprised to find that there were already about a dozen people there, ready and waiting. It was impressive to me that people had come early, but what really got my attention was the fact that they were all sitting in the front row! As more people arrived, the room filled up from the front. The price of arriving late was that you had to sit in the back! And when the chairs were all full, latecomers didn't stand in the back of the room, they came down front and sat on the floor — as close as they could get to the speaker.

I must tell you that I have worked with other groups in which the exact opposite happened. The room filled up from the back, the price of being late was that you had to sit down front, and if there weren't chairs, latecomers would stand against the back wall.

Different behavior because of a different attitude!

How do you feel about the learning process? Do you have a personal library of self-improvement books? Do you listen to educational cassettes as you drive in your car or as you jog? When you attend a training program or class do you head for the front row so that you can get the best possible return on the time you are going to invest?

When people stop learning, they've started dying. Decide right now that one of your most important qualities is your vital interest in learning and growing and becoming what you can be!

Here's key number two. Certainly not in order of importance, because this next attitude is probably the foundation of excellence in a human system. It's called "self-esteem."

My definition of self-esteem is your feeling of worthiness, value and significance as a human being. It's different from self-confidence — knowing that you can do something. Self-esteem is the degree to which you are in the habit of acknowledging the fact that you really are a very worthwhile person.

Your self-esteem got started when you were a small child. You got a lot of messages from Mommy and Daddy (and other experts) about what kind of person you were. Some were positive messages — probably there were some negative ones too. What really counted, in terms of your present level of self-esteem, was how you received those messages. Since they were coming from very important "experts," you probably accepted them as "the truth." So, if most of the signals and messages were positive, encouraging and loving, they probably led to the development of a pretty high level of self-respect and acceptance. If most of the messages you received as a child were negative, then you may have made up your mind that you aren't worth much and it is perfectly normal for others to treat you badly.

Whatever your present level of self-esteem, there is a direct relationship between that attitude and the flow of your potential.

Here are some suggestions for ways in which you can reinforce and enhance your self-esteem. Whatever your present level might be, test these ideas and see what happens as your feelings of personal worth increase.

One way to enhance your self-esteem is by recalling – and re-experiencing, in your imagination – times when you have felt a sense of pride and value. Another is to give up the habit of "wallowing" in errors and failures. Instead of reliving (and thus reinforcing) events that were negative, think about how you might handle similar situations more effectively "next time" they occur.

You can also build your self-esteem by strengthening the self-esteem of the various groups of which you are a part. Your family, the department in which you work, your company or any other team that you play on. And, last but by no means least, you can build your self-esteem by giving some to another person. In fact, the more you give, the more you get! See if you can find some simple, direct ways of helping the people with whom you live and work to feel better about themselves. You will be enhancing your environment (people who feel good about themselves are easier to live with) and your own personal self-esteem will be strengthened in the process.

Ready for another key to excellence? Take a look at how you feel about pressure!

One of the very interesting patterns that we can see in top athletes, surgeons, executives – people at the top in every walk of life – is their positive attitude about pressure. They love it! See if you can learn to lean into the demands that come your way. Deadlines, financial demands, the need to adapt to changing situations, all can be seen as stimulating and positive requirements. People who have formed the habit of perceiving pressure as a positive force in their lives are in great demand and command high salaries.

Another key to excellence is the ability to find the joy in life. People who excel have an optimistic outlook, bounce out of bed in the morning with high energy and make it through each day with a good sense of humor. As a result, not only are they more fun to be around, but they are also more healthy. Positive emotions contribute to abundant physical health — negative emotions allow illness to develop.

And, last but by no means least, is the key to excellence that I like to call personal responsibility. It's defined as the degree to which a person is comfortable (or even excited) about the fact that he/she is accountable for the consequences of his/her behavior. People who excel know that to be the case, and wouldn't have it any other way. As a direct result of that attitude, the high-performer is in the habit of reinforcing what works — and correcting for what doesn't.

People who are low on this scale do neither of those. When things go well, the non-responsible person "thanks his lucky stars." And when things go badly that person looks for someone to blame. Neither of those actions has any chance of making subsequent behavior any more productive. Notice how this quality applies to the productive people you know — and to the failures, too. Whenever possible, remind yourself that life is a series of choices, all choices and decisions have consequences and success in life is largely a matter of anticipating the positive and negative consequences of any decision and thus increasing the probability that a decision or choice will, in fact, take you in the direction that you really want to go..

Try this idea . . .

For the next week focus your attention each day on one of the five keys to excellence that we have reviewed. Start the day with the determination that you are going to expand yourself today in this one specific area. As the day progresses, look for opportunities to practice the positive attitude. Observe it in other people to see what effect it is having on their success. At the end of the day, check your progress. Were you able to put that releasing idea to work and let your potential flow more easily and more productively? Then, before you go to sleep, remind yourself of what you are going to be focusing on tomorrow.

At the end of the week you'll see the beginning of some important changes, then start back with number one and work on the five keys for another week.

I believe that you will find the process very exciting and rewarding as you become more and more able to get out of the way and let yourself grow!

2

PASSPORT TO POTENTIAL

Danny Cox
17381 Bonner Drive
Tustin, CA 92680
714/835-4353

I spent ten years of my life flying super sonic fighters. After ten years, I finally realized that the Air Force was not going to use any of the wonderful suggestions I had made on how to improve their organization. The opportunity came along to shake those people up. I sent in my resignation; they signed it, and overnight I was a civilian again trying to find out what I was going to do with the rest of my life. I had no money saved up and no retirement.

I headed for the west coast to fly with the airlines, believing they would be tickled to death to get hold of me. (As a matter of fact, they did love my qualifications... they just couldn't stand my specifications. Over the phone they'd get all excited about my flying time and all the kinds of flying I'd done. I then had to explain to them that there was one more thing I should ask them about. I said, "What are the height requirements to fly with your airline?" They said, "Five feet, eight," and I said, "That's my goal, to be five feet eight."

And I'm still working on it. I could reach everything in the cockpit, that was no problem, but the airlines didn't want people leaning out in the aisles saying, "That little guy is going to fly this big airplane? You gotta be kidding." I was ready to form an antidiscrimination group. I was going to call it SPOT, which stood for Short People On Top. I was really disappointed.

I had been known as the "Sonic Boom Salesman" in the Air Force. If I could sell sonic booms to an upset, hostile audience, I should be able to sell a product or two.

For a year I was a salesperson for a large sales corporation. After a year I was made a manager. Every day, for about a year, about all I did was show up. And then they made an almost fatal mistake. They gave me the top office out of their 36 offices. I could hardly wait to get back to that top office because that's where I'd been a new salesperson that first year. You can imagine how those top people in that office, who remembered me as the new salesperson from the year before, welcomed me back as the boss. You can also imagine how they hated me because I tried to turn everybody in that office into a carbon copy of me.

Wasn't that a wonderful plan? I took that office from number one to number 36 in three months time. I knew I was in trouble. You can always tell when you're in trouble as a manager. If you get to the parking lot in the morning and find that your salespeople have arrived early and blocked the entrances with their cars, that's a bad sign. I guess it's the modern day version of circling the wagons. We had not yet had an armed revolt but we were close. I had reached the point where I was afraid to stick the keys in the ignition of my car until I'd checked all the wiring. As a matter of fact, when I got ready to go home at night I used to send my lowest producer out to start my car — just in case. That was the only incentive plan I had.

It was about this time my boss came to see me and said, "Danny, I really made a mistake by making you a manager. I feel it's only fair to let you know that I'm looking for your replacement." I said, "That's not only the shortest but the finest motivational seminar I've ever attended. I'm going to have to learn to do this." He said, "You don't have much time," and I said, "You don't know how motivated I am."

I went to work on me, not them. And I made some discoveries. I found out that salespeople get better right after the manager does. Employees get better right after the supervisor does. Kids get better right after parents do. Students get better right after teachers do and customers get better right after salespeople do. It's amazing but it's a universal principle.

I didn't lose my job and, as a matter of fact, after 120 days we were back to number one. We used that momentum and broke office records, company records and industry records. I learned some things along the way. I call them the Passport to Potential.

There are three things to do to get ready for your trip:

☆ **Learn and visualize clearly how other high achievers think and act.** That means you must read and study, listen to tapes and take somebody to lunch before somebody else eats yours, especially in today's business world. It means you're going to have to learn.

☆ **Put into practice what you know and how it works.** We can learn new things but the tendency is to go back to the office tomorrow and do what I call "repeat yesterday one more time." You've got to break from the old and try the new. You've got to build new habits. You do that with practice.

☆ **Develop the characteristics of those high achievers.** The key here is develop; you don't have to be born with the characteristics.

These are the characteristics you need for your trip. But what are the things you'll actually need for the official passport?

First, develop a high standard of personal ethics. Now more than ever we need and understand the importance of high standards of personal ethics. We see someone who doesn't have high ethics take off like a skyrocket and say,

"Wow, look at that person go. A super star in the making." But later we're saying, "What ever happened to that person we heard so much about last year?" He probably didn't have the high standards or personal ethics that are so important.

Another thing you're going to need for a completed passport is an absence of pettiness. It's so easy to get caught up in petty things in the business world today. There are right things to do and wrong things to do and great people know not only right from wrong, but they also know what is really important to the job...what's really important to their growth. Imagine receiving a memo that says, "From this moment forward, this company will no longer furnish postage. If you want to send out thank you notes to your past customers or potential customers, you now have to buy the stamps." *Isn't that a shame*? You think, "If this company thinks that I'm going to invest 25 cents in a stamp to achieve a $500 commission they have another think coming!"

It's like we said in the fighter pilot business, some die by shrapnel, some go down in flames, but most go inch by inch playing little games. We've got to play the big games. The big games are down one road from the 'Y' we stand at every day. The other road leads to a repeat of yesterday. Those are the games you've already tried. I love that one line in the movie *The Right Stuff*, where one of the pilots says, "You never know how far you can go until you push yourself too far." We've got to understand not only what pettiness is but how to do our best to make it an empty spot in our lives. We've got to understand what is important.

One other characteristic of people I've studied is stability under pressure. I think we have to develop that stability under pressure as we prepare our passports to potential. Stability under pressure allows you to become a tough-minded problem-solver. It all comes back to priorities. Back home we say it this way, "If you've got a frog to swallow, don't look at it too long. If you've got more than one to swallow, swallow the biggest one first."

I told that story one day and a man went out and bought a frog. It was an ugly fake frog that went "RIBBIT" when you pushed on it. It now sits on the desk of whoever is currently having the largest problem in the office. He says it works great because he'll come by and say, "You've got the frog. Hang in there. I've seen you handle problems before, you're good at handling problems." He says his employees are getting little motivational talks all day long.

I thought it was a great idea (we need to help employees understand that everybody is on their team; you're on their team). At the end of the month a recipient for the "Frog Swallower of the Month Award" is selected. The winner stands in front of the rest of the group and says, "Here's how the problem got started; here's how it developed; here are the things I tried that did work; here are the things I tried that didn't work."

What else will you need to complete this passport to potential? I feel that courage is important because it takes courage to prepare a Passport to Potential. We've got to be courageous, not safe plodders. It's easy for people to be careful. They'll say, "I've got to wait till everything is right." That's like waiting with one foot in the air for everything to be just exactly right before we try something new. That's like saying, "I'm going to drive all the way across the city but I'm going to wait till all the lights are green first." You wouldn't get very far would you? You'd just be sitting in the parking lot saying, "Okay, go ahead and start. They're all green. No, wait a minute, there's one way down the road that turned red. We've got to stop and wait till they're all green." For those people who say, "I've got to wait, I've got to be careful," I say, "if you're too careful nothing bad or good will ever happen to you."

You've got to do what you fear. Otherwise, fear is in charge. Fear is not a very rational thing to be calling the shots in your life, is it? That's a good philosophy for anyone, a salesperson, a manager or a parent. You've got to do what you fear, otherwise fear is in charge. It all comes back to courage.

Complete your passport with an inspired enthusiasm that is contagious. Those great people's lives that I studied inspired my enthusiasm. It was like a pilot light on a burner. You've probably got friends who are that way. You can talk to them for two minutes on the phone and for the rest of the day people say, "What's with you today?" You answer, "I talked to a friend this morning. I don't know, he just gave me a lift." What are you describing? You're describing contagious, inspired enthusiasm. I love to be around people who have this quality because they just make you feel good. If you don't have contagious, inspired enthusiasm, beware, because whatever you *do* have is also contagious.

You can develop an enthusiasm for life. I had a woman who, out of 1200 salespeople, was the top salesperson in our company. She broke every single record in the industry. I asked her, "How do you do it?" She said, "God didn't make me with an off switch." What a concept, God didn't make me with an off switch.

I work closely with Dr. Robert Schuller. I do a lot of management and leadership training for the administrative staff at the Crystal Cathedral. Bob Schuller's got it. He wears his clothes out from the inside. He and his wife were over at our house for dinner one night. Half way through that dinner I could hardly wait, I didn't know what for, but I could hardly wait. He's got it. Contagious enthusiasm.

Several years ago I was doing a program in Florida for a room of about 1,000 salespeople. I'd just gotten to the center of the stage when I saw two people walk in to the back of the room. I looked back at them and thought, "They've got what I'm going to talk about. They've got inspired enthusiasm. I can see it from the platform." I could see how the crowd was reacting to them. I made a mental note to meet those men. I met them at the break and it was the start of a beautiful friendship. I had lunch with them that day and dinner with them that night.

Any time I go to Florida, which is fairly often, I can always depend on them being there to hear that same program. They've gone through it nine times. They could probably get up and do the program themselves. I'm talking about John and Greg Rice, identical twin brothers, all two feet nine inches of them. That's three inches shorter than a yardstick. You see, they've got it. Of course, at two feet nine, even if they didn't have inspired enthusiasm I'm going to run around with them. As a matter of fact, every time we're together I put one on each side of me like bookends, and then I walk like John Wayne. They're fun to be around.

Let's take a look at four all-important words. The first word is dream. We've got to dream like never before. My dream began on the beach with my boss looking for my replacement. I had to take two days away just to get my thoughts together so I could understand just what potential I had. Dream, that's an important word.

The second word is study. Study everything you can get your hands on to make the dream come true. Study books and tapes. Take people to lunch who are better at their jobs than you are. If someone is better at some phase of the job than you are, take that person to lunch and find out how he does it.

The third word is plan. Plan your time, but time your plan. Give yourself some time pressures. It's like we say back home, "It's okay to have a tiger by the tail if you know what to do next." Or, as Evel Knievel, the great 20th century philosopher, once said, "The worst feeling in the world is to be roaring down that track, hit that ramp and going up off that ramp at 91 mph knowing you should have been at 93 mph." You've got all that time to think, "I'm going to be about two mph short at the other end."

Planning is important, but a plan was not meant to remain a plan. What's that fourth word? Action. Get it into action. Make it happen. Commit yourself to never repeating another yesterday. Don't repeat what you know doesn't work one more time. So I challenge you to never be less than your dreams. I wish you lots of green lights and blue skies.

3

CREATING THE HIGH ENERGY CLIMATE

Tom Haggai
Suite 203
209 N. Main St.
High Point, NC 27260
919/889-8962

The most difficult problem I ever had was to understand that you don't change people. My background taught me you just believed you could change people. If you just pushed a little, you *could* somehow make people change. But it finally dawned on me that this is impossible to do.

When I was born, the psychologists were saying that a child changed until he reached the fourth grade. When I arrived at the fourth grade they said, "oops!" We made a mistake and a child only changes until he is four years of age. We, of course, now realize that when a baby is born what you see is what you get! How about that deplorable prognosis!!!

The fact is, people don't change. Quite often we have heard it said, or even said it ourselves, "I used to like that person until he changed." In reality that is not true. Every person has within himself some good qualities and, unfortunately, some negative qualities. Each day in each person's life there is a vote taken as to whether the better or the worst of us wins the moment.

Some years ago a missionary arriving back to the States from India was asked about his ministry, and he related the story of one of his more recent converts. When asked how he was doing in his personal life, he responded to the missionary, "I find that within me I have a good dog and a bag dog, and they are always having a fight."

The missionary asked, "Well, which dog wins?"

"Oh, sir, that's simple — whichever dog I say, 'Sic em,' to."

The role that you and I have as leaders is to create the climate that brings forth the best qualities in people. Dr. Elton Mayo of the Harvard Graduate School of Business Administration made a study of what made an effective workforce. The testing ground was the Hawthorne Plant of Western Electric in suburban Chicago. The time period was 1927-1932. Dr. Mayo came back to his offices at Harvard, and he summed up the secret of an effective workplace, using one word. Now you must realize that this was a Harvard professor, so it's going to be difficult to understand his word. In fact, I am going to spell it out a letter at a time because I don't want you to miss it. The word is W — A — R — M.

People work effectively where people feel warm. The theory that Dr. Mayo proved was that workers tend to cluster together into informal groups in order to fill a void in their lives. The void is a person's need for companionship and cooperation. The Industrial Revolution depersonalized humanity. If Dr. Mayo was correct in 1930, think about the effect of our automated age that is beginning to utilize robotic technology. At least in the 1930's the worker might be reinforced at home while, today, fewer than 25% of our homes are traditional, meaning both parents in the home with only one parent working.

Dr. Mayo's prescription was to cultivate communication between employer and employee and to enlist in supervision those people to whom respect for other people came naturally. Supervisors were to be trained in the skills of listening, understanding and eliciting cooperation which was quite a departure from the image of the "straw boss" of that day. Dr. Mayo literally became an industrial evangelist with a simple message: Work effectiveness declines when work deteriorates into an impersonal exchange of money for labor. He used the word, Anomie, which meant that workers felt rootless, unimportant and confused by the indifference in their environment. If people become docile, they don't have to be angry to be ineffective; they just become inefficient. Curiously enough, Dr. Mayo did not use the word productivity; and it happens to be a word I resent because it has reached the translation of meaning, "I want you to work diligently to make me look good." The employees should not be concerned about making someone else look good; they should find some fulfillment in their work.

The communication tool to create this warmth is the word *praise* . . . not flattery, not "BS," but praise that can be defined as to why the person is being praised. My fourth grade teacher was Mrs. Brooks in that big school in Massachusetts I attended that had eight grades and four rooms. She taught me something valuable as a youngster. She said, "If I point my finger at you and am critical, then three fingers are pointed back at me." Well, I believe she was right but I didn't like her comment. Right at that time, I adopted a different attitude and that is, if I point a finger at you and praise you, say something gracious about you, say something honestly complimentary about you, then three fingers come back to me. Praise reflects more on you, the giver, than on the receiver. It creates energy in both of you and synergism between you.

This sounds somewhat idealistic, and some of you say, "It would be good but with this rough and tumble business climate we have, you just can't go around praising people. Tom, you are too pollyanna." Maybe so, but I don't think I'm exactly naive.

In 1975 when the 8,000 employees of the Boy Scouts of America were thrust upon me and their problems became the key of turning this $200 million-a-year institution around, I had to oversee the release of 700 of them. That was not pleasant but you can even do the tough jobs in a kind manner.

For more than three years I served as an advisor for Frank Borman, right up until the sale of Eastern Air Lines to Texas Air. There is not any industry I know that is as difficult as the airline industry. Any time any person gets discouraged in their business, I would suggest to them that they try the airline industry for size and see what can really be tough.

At IGA, when I took over the daily operation after serving as chairman for some years, it was to turn the largest independent food system in the United States (and at retail the nation's fourth largest food group) totally around.

So I don't think I am naive, nor idealistic, nor pollyanna. In fact, I believe that the firmer one is, the fairer that person can be.

Quickly you say, "I do have to be critical; but when I am critical, it is always *constructive criticism.*" How do you know that it is? Constructive criticism is never determined by the mouth uttering the words, but, rather, by the ears listening. It is the listener who determines whether your criticism has been helpful, whether it be right or wrong. I contend that you can never begin to be constructively helpful unless you have earned the right of passage and that is *praise*.

One of the people with whom I enjoy being associated in the food industry is Don Keough, president of Coca Cola. If you are around him very much, you'll hear him say, "A lot of managers focus on weaknesses. And we all have them. I think that is a fundamental mistake. You have to look at the "beauty spots." We all have those, too. When you do that, and let the person sense it, then you get all the best that is in him. And they are not demeaned or destroyed by your constantly reaching in to find their weaknesses."

Praise is not being nice to people. Praise is recognizing that people need an environment where they can be nice to themselves, where they can say, "God didn't waste his creative power when He made me."

This delicate "climate control" is something that we can

never take for granted or think it will stay at good temperature once it is established. Remember the old song, "You always hurt the one you love . . . ?" Let me bring it home . . . to my home, to illustrate the need of periodically checking the thermostat.

Buren and I are the parents of four children . . . three daughters and a son. People so often say, "Aren't you glad you have a son?"

Well, I am but my answer to them is, "Really, the son is for Mother, the daughters are for Daddy." There is that strange chemistry. My daughters . . . now three grown ladies . . . can just call up and say, "Hi, Dad," and I feel about 20 feet tall. In fact, I can't think of any negatives about them.

My three daughters enjoyed school and floated through without causing us any anxiety. However, there is an active law of compensation; and in our case, his name is Allan Haggai. What a fine young chap — 6'2" — as handsome as his mother is beautiful (and that's saying a great deal), dependable, his word is his bond. When he said he would be home, you could "make book on it." If he was going to miss his schedule, he always called for permission. He's a very committed young man; and at the top of his commitments was that he would never allow his textbooks to interfere with his education! Now this made him popular in high school. Where else, at the end of the school year, could you buy brand new books at used book prices?

So what did "Smart Daddy" do, a daddy who has been exposed to these excellent leaders? Every morning I would start the day by saying, "Son, go to school and do it right for a change." What an encouraging last word! When he would come home having messed up, my reply simply was, "I'm not surprised. I knew you would mess up."

What I didn't know was that at 1:00 p.m., he would say to his best buddy, Keith, "Hey, I've got to mess up." And when Keith asked why, he would say, "Well, Daddy told me I was going to and I don't want to let Daddy down."

Our children or our employees usually live up to the highest level of our lowest expectations. All of his privileges were taken away; and, in fact, I called neighbors to find out what privileges they had given that I hadn't given yet . . . so I might take them away even before I gave them. I was getting just that frustrated and desperate. Finally, exasperated, I went to see his principal, Sam Dockery, and told him I had a problem with Allan.

"Oh," Sam said, "He's on drugs?"

I said, "Sam, you know he's never been on drugs."

"Then he's getting drunk?"

I said, "Sam, you know he doesn't drink."

To which Sam replied, "Then what's your problem?"

"He's flunking!"

"I thought you had a problem," Sam said.

My retort — "And, yes, I thought you were an educator, too."

Sam said, "What are you doing? Are you hollering at him, threatening him?"

"You got it."

"And it's doing a great deal of good?" Sam replied.

I said, "I wouldn't be here if it were doing any good."

Sam looked at me and said, "Tom, how many times have I heard you speak?"

"At least a dozen."

"Tom," he said, "I've never heard you speak but that I didn't leave feeling better. Now why don't you practice what you preach?"

Well, that certainly cut me to the quick because that's my only claim to fame. He continued, "Allan is one of the finest young people we have on our high school campus. When's the last time you bragged about his strengths rather than magnified his weaknesses? I'm not suggesting that, if you do so, his grades will improve dramatically, nor am I even suggesting that he should go to college. After all, Tom, there have to be some bright people to organize business so the college kids will have a place to work when they graduate unemployed. But BRAG ON HIM."

I thought about that. Fairly rebuked I was; and I thought about how Allan, like his Uncle Ted, can do anything mechanical. He kept everything repaired around our house. He fixed my car after the dealer put it in his shop to complicate what had been a simple problem! He did the recording of our radio program with me before we started sending it off for syndication.

At the first opportunity, I sat down with Allan and told him that Mother and I were not hung up about his going to college but we just didn't want him to shoot his own foot. We wanted him to retain the option. I also told him that we weren't always on the same "wave length." Like his uncles, John and Ted, he was enthusiastic in weight lifting and body development whereas I played the team sports. But where he had difficulty with his languages, they had come simply to me. He liked the subjects in science where I enjoyed history and philosophy. So we began an understanding, or at least an effort to understand. More than that, our hostility was being erased. An atmosphere of warmth was replacing it.

Now I'd like to write that his grades improved dramatically. They didn't, but he graduated with his high school class; and frankly, I would have doubted that to be possible. Allan has finished college. Where? Right here at home at High Point College. Why do you think I raised three million dollars to build the library? I bought his way in!!!

Allan did take an extra semester to graduate, but yet I recall his first grading period when he came in with C's and D's. I told him that I was proud of him — and I meant it. I would have settled for D's and F's. His reply was, "But, Daddy, I can do better."

Think of how many times I had hollered at him, "Allan, you can do better!" Now when I'm bragging on him, he's telling me that he can do better.

When he came to his senior year with excellent grades, I said, "Allan, I'm so proud of you."

He said, "But, Daddy, I can still do better."

I replied, "And, yes, I'm proud of you for two reasons: (1) for what you are doing and (2) because you know you can continue to improve.

Allan didn't change. It just took a while for his dad to put him in that atmosphere of warmth; and to think I almost ruined one of the finest young men whom I've ever known.

Today he is employed by Thomas Built Buses handling their North Carolina sales . . . happily married . . . in his own home. Yet I almost missed the opportunity.

So there you have it — creating the high energy climate in the workplace is dependent upon our creative juice of praise.

The very best example I've had of this attitude was by the lady I was privileged to call MOTHER. She was the fulfillment of Abraham Lincoln's thought that God couldn't be everywhere so he gave us our mothers. At age 19 I came home from college one day, tired. It was the first time I could ever remember being tired. No, I'm not talking about being sleepy; it was one of those days when you get up feeling worse than when you went to bed. I walked into the kitchen to see my mother and said, "Mother, I'm tired."

My mother had that ability to answer a question directly. She said, "Have an orange." I don't really know how that helped, but I had six of them.

Then she said, "I want you to let me tell you something that we probably should have told you before you were 19 but Dad and I didn't want you to have any sense of obligation. The Bible says that we love God because He first loved us. We wanted it the same way — that you would love us because we deserved and earned your love. I've never told you this, but your daddy and I don't believe in birth control. John and Ted were born; baby Paul was born but later died and then I had a miscarriage. I shouldn't have become pregnant with you, but I did. The doctor said to your father, 'Now, pastor, you'd better do that which you know how to do best and I'll do what I know how to do best. I don't really think we'll be able to save either but, if so, we're going to work to save your wife.'

Tom, you were born and you lived and I lived. It was a miracle. I've never been well but I wasn't well before you were born. I wasn't even supposed to bear you. You know, sometimes I feel a little sorry for myself. Then I begin to think about something I can do for someone, a word of praise or a word of help. Son, it's surprising but all of a sudden there comes some adrenaline you didn't even know you possessed."

My mother lived to be 80 years old. Let me tell you what I remember most about Mildred Steere Haggai. It sounds almost too fictitious to be true. *In 48 years I never heard her complain once. Never once.* The last time she was sick in Atlanta, Georgia, I called and said to her that I was so sorry that she was sick. She told me that she was sorry that I had to be sorry. She never complained once.

After Mother left us, I asked if I could look at her diary, not to be nosey but just to have greater understanding into this marvelous lady. She kept meticulous financial records since we had to live very modestly for Dad and Mother had given their lives to the gospel ministry; and the oath of poverty is not an exclusive of my Catholic friends. By simply dividing the money that she recorded each day for postage, I realized that she had averaged writing three letters a day during her lifetime, handwritten letters covering every inch of a page because she wanted to get the full benefit of her 3 cent stamp. These were "pick-me-up" notes to cheer someone she had met through the ministry that she and Dad shared.

My doctor of over three decades looked after Mom when she visited me in North Carolina; and he told me that genes, of course, are important. Yet more important than cholesterol and the other things that we speak so much about is one's attitude. My mother lived because she believed God created people to live, and she believed that you only live while you help others to live. She did, by giving her life, find her life.

Now maybe what I said about Mom sounds too noble for us; but we have roles of responsibility. We are in leadership. My suggestion is that while everybody is talking about America's declining manufacturing and our loss of creativity, I suggest that it is not our imbalance of trade . . . it is not whether our dollar be weak or strong. It comes down to what we all know — people make the difference. Our obligation is to create the high energy climate. Praise becomes our thermostat.

4

PRODUCTIVITY THROUGH MOTIVATION

Don Hutson
P.O. Box 172181
Memphis, TN 38187-2181
800/647-9166

Have you noticed that you never see a mule running in the Kentucky Derby? A stringent task is for a stringent achiever, isn't it? What about our level of personal motivation? What about our level of personal productivity? We need to stop and think about the way we have our minds set on what we want to accomplish in our given period of time on God's green earth. Sometimes we need to erase our barriers and see things in a more positive and vibrant perspective. What is your mind set? Whatever we think we're going to accomplish is what we're usually going to accomplish! Isn't that true? It's all a matter of perspective.

On his death bed J. Paul Getty was asked in an interview, "Mr. Getty, you're one of the richest men in the world, but I must ask you at this moment just one question. If you had your life to live over, what would you do differently?"

And J. Paul Getty, without even a pause, said, "Oh, that's an easy question to answer. I'd go for bigger deals." A billionaire at his death. It's a matter of our mind set. So often the perspective that we have is going to influence our level of motivation.

I happen to believe there's a correlation between the commitment we have to a cause and the achievement we experience; between motivation that we have and energy that we enjoy. The greater and the deeper our level of commitment, the more energy we will have. It will become internalized for us. It becomes a natural thing. Have you ever heard about the kamikaze pilot who flew 188 missions? He was busy but he wasn't committed. There are a lot of people who are busy but are not committed. They are simply not getting the job done.

In working with organizations throughout the world, I've had the privilege of working with some very high achievers who are very motivated people. I've also looked at some people who, with all their potential, weren't doing very well. Have you seen people like that? Maybe you even know some in your very own organizations or families. You know who I'm talking about—the kind of person who projects an image that he just likes to arrive without having made the trip. Our great challenge is to understand motivation and productivity. The late Bob Bale was a master of understanding motivation, especially as applied to the concepts of achievement. I was with Bob at our National Speakers Association convention in Phoenix many years ago. We were chatting and I said, "Bob, I've got to get your opinion on something I'm curious about. You're recognized as one of the true experts on human motivation. Bob, I want your definition of motivation. Would you share it with me?" He said, "Don, I'd be glad to give you my definition of motivation and you're welcome to use it until you find a better one." That was many years ago and I've never heard one half as good, much less any better. Bob Bale said motivation is "an idea, emotion, or need from within a person which incites or compels that person to act or not to act." The key words in that definition are the words "from within." All motivation is self-motivation. I'm convinced of that.

Years ago I was doing a management seminar for about 500 people in Atlanta in the ballroom of the Downtown Marriott. I was down front in the room preparing my visuals and getting ready for my presentation. I thought I was in the room by myself and all of a sudden, out of the corner of my eye, I spied a man walking down the center aisle toward me. This individual had on tennis shorts, tennis shirt, sweatbands around the forehead and wrists and a tennis racket in his hand. I couldn't imagine where he was going! He walked up to me and said, "You must be Don Hutson who's going to conduct the seminar for our company this morning." I said that was correct. He said, "Don, I don't know if you're aware of it or not, but at your management seminar this morning, attendance is not mandatory; it is voluntary and I'm not coming." I told him that was fine. But he was here for some reason and I was curious what it was. I asked if there was something I could do for him. He said, "As a matter of fact there is, Don. You see, I'm running my branch and I'm doing a pretty good job. We're well ahead of last year and we're pleased and proud of our performance and our productivity so far, but we're not number one. I only wanted to ask you a simple question so I thought I'd come down a few minutes, get your answer and still make my tennis date at nine o'clock." I told him I would help him if I could. "All I want to know is," he said, "how can I motivate my people?" I said, "Oh, is that all you want to know?" He said, "Yeah, that's all." I said, "You can't. Have you got any other questions?" That response intrigued him to the extent that he elected to stay for the seminar.

I learned from Bob Bale and my personal experience in sales training that you don't directly motivate another person. Motivation is accomplished through an indirect process. If we're going to motivate a customer to buy, if we're going to motivate our spouse to respond the way we want them to, if we're going to motivate anybody — we don't do it directly, we do it indirectly.

How do we achieve that? We achieve that by creating an environment and atmosphere around them that will serve as an inducement for them to motivate themselves. If you get but this one idea, it can be an idea that can change your life and the lives of those people you touch. That one idea is that all motivation is self-motivation. Don't wait on somebody else to motivate you. We're all on the periphery of greatness just for living in a free society. We've got to motivate ourselves to get out there and make it happen.

My favorite story on motivation is the one of the boy who was on his way to baseball practice. He had a coach who wouldn't tolerate tardiness. Unfortunately, the little boy was running late. He could see the baseball field some 300 yards away but he couldn't go straight to it because between where he stood and the baseball field was a large fenced pasture that contained the meanest, largest bull in the country. The little boy realized he couldn't go through the pasture; he'd have to go all the way around it. He would undoubtedly be late and be severely disciplined as a result. He was about to start walking around when, all of sudden, he looked down and saw that the old bull appeared to be sleeping. He thought if he could get over the fence and all the way across to the other side before the old bull woke up, he'd be on time for the game. He knew if he went for it he'd have to make it all the way across the pasture because there was nothing in the center of that pasture for protection but one very large tree with its lowest branch 18 feet off the ground. He was a gambler so he thought he'd go for it.

He sneaked over the fence and took off. Have you ever tried to run and tiptoe simultaneously? Well, that's what he was doing, running and tiptoeing. He looked back to check his progress and the bull was not only awake but it was chasing him! Needless to say, he was motivated. He looked back and saw that bull charging after him like locomotive. As the boy sprinted across the pasture, he could feel the ground rattling. He looked back again and there was that bull not 15 feet behind him and gaining. Perspiration was pouring off the young boy's forehead. He looked back one more time and there was that bull now not 18 inches behind him. He could feel that bull's breath right on the back of his neck. He knew he was never going to make it to the other side of that pasture but he was almost to the tree with the 18 foot limb. He looked at that 18 foot limb with apprehension but with motivation. He could still feel that bull right behind him. Even though that limb was way up there he knew he had to go for it. With all the motivation he could muster, the kid leaped up in the air for that 18 foot limb. He missed it . . . but he caught it coming down! It just goes to show that with the proper intensity of motivation we can reach incredible heights!

If we're going to motivate ourselves sufficiently, we need to clarify the objective of motivation. The obvious object of motivation is for us to achieve something productive as a result of that inner energy and desire we feel. You see, to feel motivation and not to take action is the greatest waste in the whole world. I've always heard that the average human being functions on 16 to 18% of his or her brain power. That tells me that we have incredibly powerful, untapped resources of talent and abilities within the minds and bodies of each of us. What is our job? To tie into that source of power and motivation and not to look for it externally. Let's do it to ourselves. We are at the helm of our own ship.

People often say things like, "Don, you know motivation's fine and good, but motivation doesn't last." I have an interesting rebuttal to that. A bath doesn't last either, but it's a good idea to take one once in a while. It doesn't *have* to last forever. When we experience that process, that feeling of motivation, it can energize us and make us get out there and make positive things happen.

What is a deterrent to motivation and productivity? Often times one deterrent is yourself. You say, "Well, it's easy for all those other people to be motivated and fired up, but for me it's tough. For me things don't always go just right." Things don't go just right for anybody. You see, our success is not determined by how much crow we can eloquently dish out. Our success is determined by how much crow we're willing to eat! How much rejection can you experience?

Perhaps you experience a situation where you interact with somebody and it doesn't go very well. When you have that experience, when you get rejected by another individual, what does it do to you? Does it ruin the rest of the day, the week, a month or two or your career maybe? There are some people who handle rejection very poorly. But the real pro in any given situation is the individual who experiences rejection and negative events and in the next split second is as good as he's ever been. The proverbial water off the duck's back concept . . . they don't let it get to them; they function from a posture of confidence. They believe in their own ability to get out there and make something happen with an internalized force of motivation. There are some people who handle that motivational process so poorly that they just can't motivate themselves after rejection. Why do you think movies are open in the daytime? They're for people who have just been rejected.

So we're going to motivate ourselves. What is the desired result? The desired result of that internalized motivation is greater achievement and higher productivity. Have you ever had a slump in production at whatever you do? Everybody has slumps. Everybody's individual productivity is cyclical. We all have peaks and valleys. I hope you never have another slump, but if you ever do, I'm going to give you a couple of tools and techniques that will help you get out of that slump. Can you use that? Maybe you will never have to experience a long term slump for the rest of your life. Maybe you will make more money than you've ever made before.

Here's an equation I'd like to share with you. It's called the productivity equation. The equation is Skill x Effort = Productivity. Let me give you some examples on how this equation can work. The first example is the person who is relatively unproductive. His production in the last six months would probably best be described by management as underwhelming. He possesses only one half a unit of skill. In other words, when it comes to the required knowledge to be good at what he's doing, he has a deficiency. The interesting thing is that when this deficiency is there, most people know it.

Now what does this do to the human psyche? How is he going to feel about himself? A lack of confidence is the most easily detectable negative attribute a person can have. We've got to function from that posture of confidence. This person doesn't muster confidence because he doesn't have the skills. But skills are always available. We can always learn skills. The people who don't have skills are so often the people who have not been diligent enough in their quest for skills. It's out there for us if we want it badly enough.

Predictably, this type of person will possess only one half a degree or unit of effort as well. This is an example of the relatively unproductive person. They're not fired up, so they experience a reluctance to work diligently. So in this equation we're obviously equaling one fourth a unit of productivity. This person is ineffectual. It's tough to get fired up when one doesn't know what he's talking about!

Now let's go to the average producer. We're going to say that the average producer is the person who possesses one unit of skill, puts forth one unit of effort and creates one unit of productivity. He is average across the board. So that's acceptable.

But let's also talk about the superstars. The true achievers. The true achievers are the people who are most diligently seeking ideas and skill building concepts and techniques. Extraordinarily high producers, those achievers, the people who have a very high skill factor, usually are a result of the fact that they have a hunger for knowledge and excitement for information that is unparalleled when compared to their peers. These people might well possess two units of skill.

What happens to these people psychologically? They feel good about where they are. They're confident and they're competent. So often these are the people who are out there eager to put forth the effort. In fact, they are often putting forth two units of effort, working twice as hard as the average person is working and creating four units of productivity which is, ironically, 16 times greater than our first example. So this is a geometric and very positive force.

But, these numbers don't have to be the same horizontally. For example, there might be a person in your business, industry or profession who is a true encyclopedia of knowledge. You name it, he knows it. He possesses three units of skill. He's got his proverbial act together in terms of true knowledge and ability to perform. But he's got a problem. You see, in addition to being so skillful, he's also well-intentioned. He goes home at night and sets the alarm for five o'clock the next morning. He jumps out of bed when the alarm goes off, clapping his hands and almost bumping his head on the ceiling because he's so fired up. He possesses vigor and motivation. He goes charging into the bathroom to shower and shave. He catches a glimpse of himself in the mirror and is captivated. He gets in front of the mirror and says, "You are absolutely fantastic; you are a high producer; you can really make it happen." He's got all these great intentions. The only problem is he then goes back to bed.

You see, if the effort factor is zero, we all know that zero times anything is Zero. Isn't that a sad state of events? Here's an individual who has everything in the world going for him or her except a willingness to put forth the effort. It's like dragging a ball and chain around for his entire life. We've got to put forth effort; we've got to implement and utilize our skills. When the effort is not there, the productivity is not going to be there either. It's a self-imposed limitation. In training we refer to these people as those who are inflicted with the *mineral disease* which denotes an excess of lead in certain parts of the anatomy.

May I put everything in capsule form for you? May I suggest to you that in terms of motivation we've got to accept the fact that it's an emotion, idea, or need from within us which incites us to act or not to act. We've got to take responsibility and accept the fact that we are accountable for our own productivity. It's not an external thing; we can't rely on others; it's up to us individually. That's one of the greatest benefits of living in a free society, but it's also your responsibility as a member of that free society, is it not?

I would like to suggest to you that today and in the future, you think about the fact that we create and control our own level of motivation. We can be productive to the extent that we arm ourselves with the skills and that we motivate ourselves to put forth the effort. If you do that, and do that consistently, I promise you a highly productive future.

5

THE WINNING
EDGE OF
EXCELLENCE

Jim Tunney
P.O. Box 1500
Carmel-By-The-Sea
CA 93921
408/659-3200

I travel around the country making presentations to corporations, associations and businesses both large and small. The question I'm asked most as a national football referee is why do I do it? Why would I, with a Doctorate in Education, a former superintendent of schools and Principal of high schools, walk out in the middle of 80,000 screaming and yelling people? Because it's exciting?

I referee professional football games not because it's exciting, but for two reasons. Number one, I like to be associated with winners, champions and heroes.

Number two, when I do my job on Sunday afternoon I get to work with the best people in the world at what they do. Nobody else plays football better than the people in the National Football League. Every Sunday afternoon for 20

weeks out of every year for 28 years, I get a chance to work
with the best, people like O.J. and Roger Staubach.

What is it that makes O.J., O.J. or Roger Staubach, Roger
Staubach? What is this thing called motivation? What do we
mean by excellence? How do we work to achieve peak
performance and then maintain that level of our best level?
Think for a minute, if you will, what is it that motivates you?
What is it that gets the best out of you? What motivates
you?....love of work? recognition? The fact that you've done
a good job and people recognize you for it makes you feel
good and makes you want to do it even better. What
else?....pride? You feel good about yourself, you're proud of
your work. What else? What about accepting the challenge of
excellence?

Let me tell you what motivates me. June motivates me.
The month, not the woman. Because in that month each year
I have the privilege of working with the California State
Special Olympics. Every June 3,200 mentally and physically
handicapped young kids compete in the same Olympic
events that our champions compete in. I saw an 11 year old
girl win the three meter diving championship. She was blind.
I saw a kid in a wheelchair with cerebral palsy so bad he had
no use of either hand or of one leg. But he could reach the
ground with his other foot, so he pushed his wheelchair
backward in the race. He won it and was ecstatic with his
accomplishment. I saw a 26 year old, mentally, physically and
emotionally handicapped young man standing on the victory
stand because he had just won in his age category the
hundred meter dash. When the judge pinned the ribbon
around his neck with that gold medal hanging there this
young man said, "Thanks." I was standing not far away. I
turned to say something to the sponsor and tears were rolling
down her cheeks. I said, "You know, that's a marvelous
accomplishment for that young man." "Yes," she replied.
"That's the first word he's ever spoken."

How do we get the best out of ourselves? What is it that
makes you want to be excellent at what you do? Oliver
Wendell Holmes said it a long time ago. "Most of us die with

our music still in us." How do we get the music out? How do we get to the potential that is there? What is it that makes some people want to be the best? I believe, in a word, it's *power*. Yes, power. I think power motivates people. But I call it personal power — as opposed to, say, position power.

You know position power if you were ever in the military service. Generals have it. In the school business, teachers, principals and superintendents sometimes have it. It comes from the position that you hold.

Personal power, on the other hand, has nothing whatsoever to do with what other people say you are. It has nothing whatsoever to do with what you say you are. Personal power comes out of who you are all the time. I happen to believe the more personal power that you take into any relationship the less vulnerable you'll be to those working out of their position power. There is power present in all relationships. Husband/wife, mother/daughter, father/son, teacher/student, employer/employee and superior/subordinate.

As a referee I've got to have power. But I've got to have personal power, not position power. Even after 28 years in the NFL and three Super Bowls, I can't walk out onto that football field and say, "I'm the referee and you better pay attention to me." That would last about five minutes then they would run me right out of the stadium. On the other hand, I refuse to be intimidated by any player, any coach, any stadium, any spectator. I'm going to do my thing. If they like it, that's swell. If they don't, well I'll find a stadium that does.

It comes from the feeling of self-confidence. How is your level of self-confidence today? Do you feel good about yourself? Do you feel good about what you do? Do you feel good about your relationship with an employer or an employee? Do you *really* feel good about what you do? Self-confidence is vital to what you do. Of all the things that I have read, studied or researched about self-confidence, Ralph Waldo Emerson said it best. He said, "Man surrounds himself with the image of himself." Yes, people surround themselves with the image of themselves. That has two meanings to me. Number one, it's very important that you have self-confidence. Look at it this way. You go to buy a product like a television, washing machine or automobile and you want that salesperson to have knowledge of their product and an ability to sell it to you. You want them to sell you on the value and benefits of that product to you. That's why you're there. That salesperson needs to be open, communicative and honest with you. That's what you want from a salesperson.

How do *you* deal with people? Do you really feel good about it? Do you really feel good in terms of your selling? Do you feel good in terms of dealing with a child in your family or a spouse? It's not a feeling arrogance, it's not saying I'm better than you and I don't have to deal with you. Arrogance turns people off. I'm talking about self-confidence. Self-confidence says that I feel so good about myself that there is ample to help you with a problem that you have. It's a feeling that comes from abundance. Excellence comes from abundance.

Feeling good about yourself is vital to what you do. It's very important in today's world as we manage people..... and incidentally we all manage people, not in terms of manipulation or intimidation, but in terms of leadership, of love. As we manage people, it's important that we raise the confidence level of the people we manage. The days of the boss or supervisor who pushes people down when they make a mistake are gone. We find now that to increase productivity we must raise the confidence level of people that we manage. How do you raise the confidence level of others if you don't have it within yourself? It's important that you build the confidence level of other people, particularly when they make a mistake. That doesn't mean to sweep the mistake under the rug. What it means is to deal with the mistake in a positive way.

We all want to succeed. In my 27 years in education, I've never met a child who wanted to fail. People want to succeed. Are you willing to use your ability and your self-confidence to deal with them and help them to believe in themselves? Do you believe in what you do? Do you believe in you?

That's kind of a strange word, belief. Do you believe in God? Most people would say they do. Well, that's nice, I do too. But, why? Do you know God? Ever seen him? Can you draw me a picture? Interesting, we believe in someone that we can't see or can't touch, but we don't believe in ourselves, someone that we nurture, we clothe and we bathe every day. When we fail, have that temporary setback and get knocked down, we say, "I can't make it." Life is so . . . daily. That's right, it takes place every day.

When I was Superintendent of Schools, life was a little difficult sometimes as I carried out my duties. I heard that one of our fifth grade teachers asked her students to draw something that was interesting and exciting to them. She gave them a few minutes and moving around the room, came to this little girl. She said, "Patricia, what are you drawing?" Patricia said, "I'm drawing a picture of the city, teacher. San Francisco is such an exciting city. It's so exciting to me." The next little boy was Charlie and the teacher asked him what he was drawing. He said, "I'm drawing a picture of the airplanes. Some day I'm going to fly jet planes off an aircraft carrier." Way back in the corner was a kid named Ty. Ty has his head buried in the paper and was working very hard. The teacher asked him what he was drawing. He said, "I'm drawing a picture of God." She said, "But nobody knows what God looks like." Ty kept on working and said, "They will in a minute."

Interesting that we believe in something we can't see and can't touch, but yet we don't believe in ourselves. You say, "Okay, Tunney. I know what you're talking about. I hear you motivational guys going around the country saying every day is a great day!" Well, every day is a great day. You don't believe that every day is a great day? Just try missing one. Lots of problems, lots of tasks, but also lots of opportunities.

The Rev. Jesse Jackson said, "It's not your aptitude but your attitude that determines your altitude if you have intestinal fortitude." Attitude is so vital to what you do. When I think about that I think about a man named Victor Frankel who wrote, *Man's Search For Meaning*. That's what it's all about in this world, a search for meaning. Dr. Victor Frankel was an Austrian psychiatrist who was incarcerated in

Auschwitz concentration camp during World War II. Frankel survived it and wrote *Man's Search For Meaning*. He said, "You know, of all the freedoms you have, and of all the freedoms that can be taken away from you, the one freedom that no one can take away from you is the freedom to choose the attitude with which you approach any problem, task or opportunity." No one controls that attitude but you.

You see it all the time. Somebody says, "Well, I'm not a morning person. I'm kind of grouchy till I've had my first cup of coffee. My Dad was that way and his Dad. It's sort of a family thing." If you want to be grouchy in the morning, that's your privelege. But, don't blame it on a cup of coffee or dear old Dad. Your ability to chose what you want your attitude to be is vital to what you do. You can change from the negative to the positive.

How does it work? "You gotta accentuate the positive and eliminate the negative. Latch on to the affirmative and don't mess with Mister In Between," as Johnny Mercer wrote. That song was very popular when I was in high school. I loved music when I was in high school, but I also loved athletics. I wanted to be a baseball player. I wanted to pitch for the New York Yankees. I wanted to stand in Yankee Stadium, the house that Ruth built, and pitch off that mound. I couldn't break a pane of glass from across a small room. I just didn't have it. But I played baseball in high school for four years.

I better be honest with you. I didn't play a lot, I sat on the bench a lot. But I was one of those guys who was there every day. I never missed a day of practice. I figured they couldn't have a day of practice if I wasn't there. I sat on that bench for a long time. But when I got to be a senior, I was the starting second baseman of the Alhambra High School baseball team. Now that's probably not too important to you, I understand, but it was to me. Boy, I felt good. I figured the coach put me over on second base because he knew in high school baseball most of the hitters are right handed and their going to hit to third and short. I'd do less damage as a second baseman. So I was the starting second baseman. We were playing El Monte High School. El Monte High and Alhambra were tied for the league championship. We wanted to win it. I remember the day so well. Friday afternoon. We were at El Monte, bottom of the ninth. The bases were loaded, but we were ahead three to two. There were two outs...get the picture? El Monte was up and I'm the second baseman. Quietly I said to myself, "Don't hit the ball to me." I thought all they had to do was hit that ball to me, the ball would go between my legs, two runs would score and who would they blame? Tunney. I thought about that. That was the voice of a loser. I didn't want to be a loser, I wanted to be a winner. How did I turn that around?

When I went to college the next year, I was the starting first baseman on our Occidental College baseball team. We had a good team, we went 23 and 2. During every game, every inning, every pitch, I remember saying to myself, "Hit the ball to me." I didn't want to be the hero or star. I just knew I could make the play.

How about you? Can you make the play? Is there a task that is too big, too tough for you? Or is it something you can handle? I can handle it, give it to me. I know I can do it. Is "I can do it" part of your vocabulary? Do you say, "I feel good about myself. If I do get knocked down I still will believe in what I do."

It's the attitude that I can make it, I do have that opportunity. I have the capacity to do it. Capacity. Oh, we hear it all the time. You and I have both said it. "That team won because they played over their heads." What does that mean? "Over their heads?" One might play beyond his normal performance or better than he'd played in the past. What is your limit? Do you set limits for yourself? Do you set limits for the people you manage? Do you set limits for your children? Are there boundaries? There are no limits to what you can do. Knowing you *can do it* is vital to what you do. Think of yourself as being the best you can be and see yourself as a winner.

Peter Drucker said it very well. He said, "The only way to predict the future is to create it." Are you creating your future? Do you make things happen?

6

THE ROLE OF A MANAGER

Ken Blanchard
125 State Place
Escondido, CA 92025
(619) 489-5005

Stories about bad managers abound. In fact, bad mangers have been shown to make people sick. My wife Margie wrote a book with Mark Tager entitled WORKING WELL. What they were trying to find out was what made a healthy work environment. One of the questions they asked people was: "Can a bad boss make you sick?" What do you think poeple said? "You're darn right!" People attributed ulcers, migraine headaches, stress and similar ailments to poor managers. You can talk to somebody at one moment and they will tell you how happy they are at work. See them two months later and they might be down in the dumps, depressed, and un-motivated about work. In many cases they have gotten a new boss. And what kind of boss is that? A boss who doesn't appreciate them, jerks them around and treats them as if they were office furniture.

Why do bosses behave like that? Why is the Number 1 style of management in America what I call "seagull management"?

Seagull managers fly in, make a lot of noise, dump on everybody and fly out. I think the main reason why managers do this is that they can't understand the purpose of being a manager, that is, the "management paradox" as two of my associates — Rick Tate and Gary Heil — call it.

Most organizations are typically pyramidal in nature. Who's at the top of the organization? The chief executive officer, the chairman, the board of directors. Who's at the bottom? All the employees — the people who do all the work. The people who make the products, sell the products, service the product and the like. Now there is nothing wrong with having a traditional pyramid for certain tasks. The paradox is that the pyramid needs to be right side up and upside down depending on the task.

It's absolutely essential that the pyramid stay upright when it comes to setting major goals, vision, mission, values and the like. Moses did not go up on the mountain with a committee. Direction in organizations has to come from the top. Department chairmen have to set the vision and direction for their people. Where you get in trouble with the pyramid mentality, though, is when it comes to implementation. If you keep the pyramid right side up when it comes to accomplishing goals and visions, now you have a problem. When the pyramid is right side up, who do you work for? The person above you. The minute you think you work for the person above you, you are assuming that person — your boss — is *responsible* and what your job consists of is being *responsive* to that boss and to his or her whims and wishes.

I talk to people all the time, and they tell me the worst thing that can happen to you is to lose a boss, particularly one you have just figured out. Because then you have to go about figuring out a new other boss and how what he or she wants differs from your last boss. People think their career depends solely on their quality of relationship with their bosses. As a result, the most important people in your organization — those individuals who have contact with your customers — spend all their time looking over their shoulder trying to figure out what their boss is doing rather than focusing their attention on the customer. Why? Because their boss is usually about to hit them. The American way of managing is if you do something right, nobody says anything. If you screw up, they hit you. We call that the "leave alone-zap" style of management.

Nobody objects to vision, direction and values coming from the top of the organization. But when it comes to implementing goals and visions if the pyramid remains right side up all of the energy and attention continues to flow back up the pyramid away from the customers. As a result, you get those people who have customer contact responding to requests by saying things like "I'm sorry. We can't do that. It's against our policy." And the customer says, "What do you mean it's against your policy? It's a stupid policy." And the reply: "I'm sorry. I just work here. They don't pay me to think. I leave the brains at the door and pick them up at the end of the day."

You have all kinds of responses like that. Why does this occur? Because the energy of the organization is going up away from customers. People are defending policies rather than serving customers. Let me give you a couple of specific examples.

One of my colleagues tells a story about a customer relations situation. This associate loves ice cream. One day while he was running errands he got an "ice cream attack" so he pulled into one of the local ice cream shops in San Diego. You know, the kind of place that has 33 flavors. He went in and the young girl behind the counter says, "May I help you?" My friend said, "Let me think about what I want." While he was thinking, an older woman came behind this young girl and whispered in her ear. When he looked up the young girl said, "You'll have to take a number."

Now there was nobody else in the store. My friend said, "You've got to be crazy. Why would I have to take a number? Nobody else is in the store." And sure enough she said: "It's our policy." He said, "Well, it's a stupid policy when there's nobody else in the store. I can see it when you've got a big crowd here, but this is ridiculous." The young girl lowered her voice and went quickly to her last line of defense. "Please don't get me in trouble. She's my boss." The older woman had gone to the other side of the store. He said, "This is so absurd I'm going to have to go along with it." So he took a number, which was 30. Now luckily the number behind the counter was only 27. So here is this poor gal with nobody else in the store shouting "27! 28! 29! 30!" and then finally, "Can I help you?" He said, "I'm no longer hungry."

How do you think the girl felt? What kind of self-esteem did she have? She knew that she was implementing a stupid policy for that particular circumstance. And yet, where was her energy focused? With the customer or with her boss? Clearly, with her boss. My friend went over to the boss as he was leaving the store and said, "That's the most ridiculous thing I've ever seen — having a customer take a number when nobody else is in the store." The boss looked at him with a sarcastic look and said, "If I don't get them to obey the policies when there is nobody in the sore, how do you think I'm going to get them to do it when there is a real crowd in here?"

I had a similar experience in Hawaii not long ago. I was there giving a seminar and I called the golf course near our hotel to make a tee off time for after the seminar. I told the man in the pro shop that we would like to tee off at four o'clock. He said, "Fine." I said to him, "How long does it stay light?" He said, "It doesn't matter." I said, " What do you mean it doesn't matter?" He said, "The golf carts have to be in at 6:15." I said, "But how late does it stay light?" He said, "You don't seem to understand. The carts have to be in at 6:15 because they have to be on the battery charger by 6:30." Since it was June, I knew it stayed light until sometime between 8:00 and 9:00. I left confused.

The next day when the seminar was over people wanted to talk to me and my wife, and I didn't get over to the course until 4:30. They would not let us on the course. They said, "The last group goes out at 4:00. It takes about two hours to finish a round and the carts have to be in at 6:15." I said, "Well, can't we just go out and play a few holes?" He said, "We start the sprinklers right after the last group." I said, "Well, is there any way we can go around the sprinklers?" He said, "No. If you do and get wet or something, you're going to sue us." Now my wife, who is much better in these situations, went over to the attendant and, using all of her human relations skills including patting him on the hand, said, "Could we do a little problem solving? We'd like to play just a few holes. How could we do that?" He shouted, "Tomorrow!"

Now the first reaction to this kind of treatment is to blame the attendant. But as we saw in the ice cream example you can't blame the attendant. You have to look at the organization's management. Why do people hold on to silly policies when they don't make any sense for the customer? Because if they don't follow the policies they are going to get beaten up by their boss. The most popular leadership style in America is what we call "bicycle leadership." Bicycle leadership is when you bend your back to those above while you trample those below. I'll never forget that the cover of *THE SATURDAY EVENING POST* one time had a beautiful example of bicycle leadership. The first frame showed a guy being chewed out by his boss. The second frame showed him chewing out his wife. In the third frame, the wife was chewing out their little son. In the last frame, the little boy was kicking the family cat.

Blaming of that type occurs when the pyramid is right side up in the traditional sense for the implementation of goals. What do you think the stated goals of most organizations are? It's to serve the customer. And yet, because of the way we organize ourselves, few companies practice effective customer relations. When it comes to implementation and goal accomplishment I feel that we have to turn the pyramid upside down.

When somebody is a guest at a hotel, buying a product or service, as a customer he or she doesn't care who is the top management of the company. The most important person in the whole organization to that customer is the person they are dealing with right then and there. In most organizations the customer contact people are not only paid the least, but they are least appreciated. Why? Because the weight of the whole organiztion is coming down on top of them forcing them to squish the customers.

You can't expect to mistreat your people and then have them be nice to your guests. In our book *THE POWER OF ETHICAL MANAGEMENT*, Norman Vincent Peale and I had a great quote from Benjamin Franklin. He said, "You can't expect an empty bag to stand up straight." What he meant by this is that people with low self-esteem can't be expected to treat others well. If you don't care for your people, how are you going to have them take care of your customers? The only way is if you give your customer contact people some breathing room. How do you do that? By turning the pyramid upside down when it comes to implementation.

When you turn the pyramid upside down, who is at the top of the orgainzation? The customer contact people. Who is *really* at the top of the organization? The customers. Who's at the bottom now? The "top" management. When you turn a pyramid upside down philosophically, who works for whom when it comes to implementation? You work for your people. This one change, while it seems minor, makes a major difference. The difference is between who is *reponsible* and who is *responsive*. With the traditional pyramid, the boss is always responsible and his or her people are supposed to be responsive to the boss. When you turn the pyramid upside down those roles get reversed. Your people become responsible and the job of management is to be responsive to their people. That creates a very different environment for implementaiton. If you work for your people then what is the purpose of being a manager? *To help them accomplish their goals*. Your job is to help them win. Let me give you a few positive examples of customer service in an organization that has the pyramid turned upside down when it comes to implementation.

The first example comes from Nordstrom, a department store chain that started in Seattle and is slowly expanding across the country. It's wiping out competition wherever it goes. In fact, in several areas I understand they are even trying to zone Nordstrom out. Why? Because they are beating everybody to the punch when it comes to customer service. My daughter Debbie, who is 21, worked last summer as a sales cashier in Nordstrom in San Diego.

After about a week on the job, I had dinner with her and asked, "What is it like to work at Nordstrom? Tom Peters and everyone is talking about Nordstrom and their tremendous service." She said, "It's very different." I asked, "What's different about it?" She said, "Well, the first thing that is different is their orientation program. Every employee has to go through an orientation program before they can start work. The whole emphasis in the first part of the program is to teach everyone, all the employees, how to say 'No problem.'" The mumber one thing they want coming out of your mouth is 'No problem.'

At Nordstom, they will take anything back that you have a problem with. One of Debbie's jobs as a cashier was taking stuff back. She said, "You wouldn't believe some of the junk people bring back." At Nordstrom the assumption is the customer is always right. In most cases they give you cash back for returns. They don't want their customers to go through all kinds of paper work. The assumption of Nordstrom's top management is that 90 percent of the poeple in America are honest and want good service for being a customer. The other 10 percent will rip you off. The problem is that most organizations are set up to stop the 10 percent minority rather than serve the 90 percent majority of honest customers.

I asked Debbie "What else is a little different about working at Nordstrom?" She said, " My boss. About three or four times a day he comes up to me and says, 'Debbie, is there anything I can do for you?' He acts like he works for me." The reality in the Nordstrom philosophy is that he does. Every manager works for their people.

We had another beautiful example involving Debbie. Her 21st birthday happened to fall during Easter week last year. That was vacation time for her at the University of Colorado.

A lot of her friends decided to go to Palm Springs. We wanted to throw a party for Debbie so we decided to have it in Palm Springs. We went to Rancho Las Palmas Marriott which is a five-star hotel. It's one of my favorite places to stay. They had a really nice room for our party, which included a disc jockey for dancing, and a bar. Fairly early in the party the waitress we had came up to Debbie and asked her what she would like to drink. Debbie asked for a Cape Cod.

Now I didn't even know what a Cape Cod was. I later found out it was vodka and cranberry juice. It turns out it's a big drink at the University of Colorado so four or five of Debbie's friends asked for one, too. I happened to be standing at the bar at the time. The waitress came up to the bartender and said, "I have an order for five Cape Cods." He said, "I don't have any cranberry juice behind the bar. Check with the kitchen." The waitress went into the kitchen and came back a few minutes later and said, "There's no cranberry juice on the property." The bartender said, "Fine. Send the bellman to a grocery store to get some." The waitress went over to Debbie and her friends and said, "I'd like to apologize. We don't have any cranberry juice on the property, but a bellman is going to the grocery store, and he'll be back in ten minutes with some cranberry juice."

Ten minutes later, the door of our banquet room opened, and there was the bellman with a case of cranberry juice. At this hotel, they give the bellman discretionary money to use for the benefit of customers and in customer service situations like this.

Now, what do you think about the self-esteem of those people? Could they solve the guests' problems? Yes! Did they have to go and talk to the supervisor in that type of situation? No! When I sent a praising letter and talked to the management about this example they were thrilled. They said that was exactly what they were trying to get their people to do.

When it comes to implementation the purpose of being a manger has got to be service. Serving who? Serving your people so that they can serve your customer. As a manager, if you don't serve your customer or you don't serve somebody who serves a customer you ought to be looking for another job. A customer is anybody who receives the results of your efforts. Customers are not only external to the organization, but can often be internal as well. In accounting, your customers are the different managers and departments that get your reports. In personnel, the customer is every employee.

In organizations, so often we don't make the switch in the direction of the pyramid when it comes to implementation. We set goals, we set dreams and then we keep the pyramid right side up for implementation. It just doesn't work well that way. What happens when the pyramid remains right side up is that the energy in the organization goes away from the customer and people start thinking that their main avenue to success is their political relationship with those people above them. When it comes to accomplishing goals the role of a manager is to serve your people. It's the leader as follower and servant.

The best way I can illustrate this role and the power of it is when it comes to performance review. When I go around the country and ask people "How many of you are thrilled with your performance review system? How many of you find it enhances self -esteem?" I hardly ever get anybody to raise their hand and say they feel good about their performance review system except some people in personnel who might have put it together.

Why don't people feel good about performance review? Because performance reviews are usually set up with the traditional pyramid mentality: The job of the mananger is to beat people up, to catch people doing things wrong. If you have a performance review system where you have a rating scale from 1 to 10 from poor performance to good if you rated everybody a 10 that reported to you, how do you think you would get rated by your boss? 2 or 3. What would they say to you? "You're too easy. You're giving away the farm." As a result, it doesn't take managers long to realize that if he rates everybody highly, he gets rated low; therefore, the only way he can get rated highly is if rates some of his people low. Now the toughest job of a manager is determining who they are going to screw.

There are three parts to an effective performance review system. *Performance planning* where you set the goals and objectives, *day-to-day coaching* where you help the people accomplish goals, and *performance evaluation* where you sit down and look over a person's performance over time. Which of those three gets done first in most organizations? In most cases performance evaluation. Personnel comes up with some damn form. Then people say, "Well, maybe we ought to have some goals around here." Then they bring in goal writers, and they write goal and job descriptions. They fill notebooks.

What is the only one of the three main parts of a performance review system that never gets done on a systematic basis? Day-to-day coaching. And yet, if we turn the pyramid upside down and make the role of the manager to serve when it comes to implementation, what is the main job of a manger? Day-to-day coaching once goals are set to help people win.

The best analogy I can give to what I'm saying goes back to my teaching career. I taught at universities for ten years. I was always in trouble. I was investigated by some of the best faculty committees. One thing that drove the faculty crazy is that on the first day of class I always gave out the final exam. The faculty would say, "What are you doing?" I'd say, "I'm confused." They'd say, "You act it." I'd say, "I thought I was supposed to teach these kids." "You are, but don't give them the questions on the final." I'd say, "Not only am I going to give them the questions on the final, but what do you think I'm going to teach them all semester? I'm going to teach them the answers because when they get to the final exam I want them to get A's." Life is all about getting A's, not some stupid normal distribution curve.

The job of a manager is to help people win. In order to do that you have to philosophically turn the pyramid upside down and recognize that your job when it comes to implementation is to help your people win. When you do that does it mean that you're setting easy goals? No way. In fact, people will set higher goals if they know their manager is committeed to helping them win. The reason people don't want to set tough goals is that they think their manager will use those goals to beat them up in a much more systematic way than they did before. My experience is that people will stretch and push themselves if they are in an environment where the manager wants them to win. Life is all about winning and that should be the role of managers. Serve your people and help them win once the goals have been set. Do that, and you'll focus on the most important role of manager!

7

A TICKET TO
ANYWHERE

Cavett Robert
1284 E. Edgemont
Phoenix, AZ 85006
602/266-2508

One of the mysteries of mankind is that we find 20% of the people in practically every line of endeavor responsible for 80% of the constructive activities and the other 80% responsible for the remaining 20%.

Why are some people creators of circumstances and others, with equal opportunity, only creatures of circumstances? Why do things happen to some people and why is it that others cause things to happen?

I hope this chapter will assist you in understanding this great mystery of life. I hope you will better realize why some people find their opportunity rather than their problem — why, to them, life is magic, not mystery, logic, not luck.

Let's Take An Imaginary Journey

One Saturday night a businessman found himself in a little town in the territory he served. His car needed repairs and he couldn't drive to his home town.

The streets were bare; there was no entertainment to be found. Very bored and somewhat cynical, he walked up to a stranger on main street and sarcastically asked, "What is this town noted for anyway?"

The local member of the chamber of commerce straightened himself up and proudly said, "My friend, you can start from this town and go anywhere in the world you want to go."

I'm not sure that he was not telling the stranger off, but in any event, it gives me a cue to invite you to take a little imaginary journey with me. Imagine that you have a little card in front of you. I suppose a card is made up of pulp, rags or wood and a few chemicals, but if you will just for a few minutes fill in this card mentally with me, I'll guarantee it can take you anywhere in the world you want to go – that is, if you really want to make the trip.

If you sincerely and voluntarily fill it out, it can be a ticket to take you anywhere in life; it can be a magic carpet that will take you to the great city of your dreams, aspirations and ambitions; it can be a key to open the door to the miracle of life with its wondrous possibilities. All of this is possible, however, only if you really want to make the trip.

Now let's examine this card and fill it out carefully.

First – What Is Our Destination?

What is the first thing we see on any ticket? Yes, it's our destination, isn't it? Where do we really want to go in life?

Some people just don't want to go anywhere. They are bogged down in complacency and are satisfied to remain there. About all we can say for these people is that we hope they vegetate silently, unobtrusively and don't affect the lives of those around them.

Just a Short Trip

Then we have those people who want to take just a little trip, they don't want to go very far. They want to hurry back to the status quo. They have built-in limitations. They want a life of quiet desperation. They flit from mediocrity to mediocrity with enthusiasm and optimism.

As for this second group of people, all we can say is that they were born in inertia and had a relapse. They don't even burn the candle at one end. They are suffering from that scientific disease that's known in technical circles as laziness.

They Advise Others in their Travels

Also, we have those people who don't want to take the trip, but they pose as experts on criticizing the travels of others. It's a "dog in the manger" situation. They are like the man who didn't kiss his wife for 30 years and finally shot the guy who did. They don't want to take the trip and they don't want anyone else to take the trip either.

The only thing we can say about these critics is that they were born in the objective case and have been walking around in the subjunctive mood ever since.

As Far as the Ticket Will Take Them

Finally, we have those people who want to go as far as the ticket will take them. They truly have the gift of dissatisfaction and divine discontent. They have hitched their hearts to a task they love — their souls are blazing with purpose and they know where they want to go.

These people are not afraid to reach for the stars. They know that even should they miss, they'll at least not come up with a handful of mud. They'd rather shoot at something and miss than shoot at nothing and hit. They are ever conscious of the fact that there is no such thing as a trip without a destination, no such thing as success without a purpose. Ever mindful are they that obstacles are only those things we see when we take our eyes off our goal. Long ago they learned that people do not fail in life because they plan to fail — they fail because they fail to plan.

Your Destination Must Be Specific

Nothing clutters up the landscape of understanding and

congeals confusion as do generalities. Specifics alone give a directional compass to life.

Do you really have a specific goal in life? What is it? Is it that you want to put your kids through college? Is it to be head of your firm — President of your company? You must have something specific you desire. If your desire is great enough, this one quality brings into focus all the other qualities within you which enable you to accomplish your specific goal.

It's a tragic fact that in our country, the greatest country in the world, if I went out and stopped the next two dozen people on the street, there would not be six who could recite a specific desire which governs their lives. And I am afraid there wouldn't be a dozen who could tell with certainty just why they went to work this morning.

And so the first thing we must insert in our ticket is our destination. Without this, there is no trip at all. Just as it's impossible to come back from some places we have never been, it's altogether preposterous to suppose that we can arrive anywhere without a place to go!

Second — What Is Our Time Schedule?

What's the next thing we see on a ticket? It's the time schedule. When do we want to go? And more important still, when do we want to arrive at our destination? Do we want to go now, from this very room, today — this moment? Or do we want to join those disenchanted people who are always putting something off until tomorrow and consequently never take the trip?

One of the unhappy circumstances of this life is that the world is full of well-meaning but misguided people who want to prepare for the future. In fact, they periodically vow emphatically that they want success enough to do something about it, and yet somehow they never get around to it. How many of these people do you know who are always about ready to commence to begin to start to do something pretty soon?

Unless you decide to go now, I guarantee you'll never take the journey. Why? I'll tell you why. There is no tomorrow. Yesterday does not exist. We live only today, right now, this very hour. Our only existence is the present.

The Magic and Miracle Of Time

Does time really have a meaning to us? Each day we have the opportunity to watch the magic and miracle of time. Time — life's most priceless tool, that which cannot be weighed in the balance or tested in the crucible. But we know it's the only ingredient that we use to transform our dreams into realities and our hopes into success.

A New Gift Each Day

Did it ever occur to you that God, in his infinite wisdom, gives time to us in such small doses that we can't too easily squander it? Every morning, when I wake up, my pocketbook is magically filled with 24 hours of this precious, priceless substance we call time. And when tomorrow comes and I know that I have given up a whole day of my life for it, I want it to be something that's good, not bad, some gain, not loss — something I can be proud of. And yet, nature is so forgiving. Even if I waste it, "each night I burn the records of the day. At sunrise every soul is born again." Again I wake up — 24 more of those non-refundable fragments of eternity that are magically in my pocketbook — just as valuable and unused as if I had not thrown the others away.

Did you ever hear a person say, "I just don't have time." What he is really saying is that there are other things more important to him. We all have a lot of time. We have all the time there is. The hands of the clock go around at the same rate of speed for everyone of us. The main thing is that sometimes we don't put importance on those things that are important. We give inconsequential matters disproportionate importance. We major in the minors and we minor in the majors.

The Trip is Now or Never

Just how valuable is your time to you? Can you afford not to start the trip today? Our time is too valuable to waste and since we know there is no tomorrow, then unless we fill in today's date on our ticket, I'm afraid that next week, next month, next year, ten years from now, honest as may be our intentions, we shall find ourselves in the wilderness of procrastination, still responding to the siren songs of complacency.

Why can't we realize that there is no other way except by starting today? Don't we feel honestly that we are worth the investment?

Starting Now is Our Only Insurance

Most people wouldn't drive their car from the garage unless it were fully covered by insurance. Practically everyone has insurance on their house. Very few people would dare to subject themselves to the dangers of everyday living without life insurance.

And yet, insurance-minded as these people may be, many of them are not insuring their futures against constant changes by starting *now* to prepare themselves to cope with those changes.

The world owes us nothing, but we owe ourselves, our loved ones and the entire world the duty to develop our God-given qualities to the ultimate. It is a great challenge and not an easy one to meet. But it's also up to us and us alone to make our dreams come true, our plans come alive.

And so, look at your ticket again. Let's make the date today — this very moment. It's the only way we can be sure to get our just share of the tasks and rewards of this life. If we don't start now, we'll never reach the great city of our ambitions and aspirations.

Third — What is Our Route?

What's next on our ticket? It's the route, isn't it? Let's not be seduced by the temptation to try the easy paths of life. Some people say that the great focal point of life is where the two highways of preparation and opportunity cross. Others call it luck. I won't argue the point but this I do know. Strength always flows from adversity. Troubles, trials and sacrifices have always constituted the fertile soil for growth. If you will take time carefully to review your life, you will realize that you make your greatest progress in life during times of discouragement and challenge. You will find that the lasting qualities of life are usually forged on the anvil of disappointment.

While no one seeks hardships, we know that they can't be avoided along the highway leading to success. Our only choice is to meet them squarely and rise above them. The road will never be easier — it is up to us to become stronger.

An Optimistic Route

Be sure that you take an optimistic route. We read so much about positive thinking these days that we are tempted to be casual in considering its importance. But please, never forget, the sweet magic of a cheerful disposition. Everyone enjoys being around an optimist.

On the other hand, a pessimist takes such a toll on us. I'd much prefer that a man steal my money than steal my optimism. The reason a pessimist is so dangerous is due to the law of emotional gravity. One pessimist can pull six optimists down with less effort than six optimists can lift up one pessimist.

Yes, we want to be kind and helpful to everyone possible, but to expose ourselves to a person with the smallpox of pessimism is a calculated risk too grave to take.

A Route of Happiness

We cannot be successful in our work or undertaking in life unless we enjoy what we are doing and feel a sense of fulfillment. Unless we are happy in what we are doing, we are a job hazard, a professional malcontent.

Years ago I was attending a convention on salesmanship. There were six or eight small meetings going on simultaneously. One that attracted my attention was labeled "The

Greatest Sale I Ever Made." I was intrigued and could hardly wait to get to the meeting. I was sure that the speaker would relate his experiences on difficult persuasion. I thought perhaps I would hear that a man 90 years old had bought a 20 year endowment life insurance policy. Maybe the speaker would relate the old cliche about selling two milking machines to a farmer with just one cow and then taking the cow in as a down payment.

What I really heard was this, "The greatest sale I ever made in my life was the day I finally bought what I was doing—the day I saw the big picture, the day I had the great concept, the great passion—when I truly began believing in what I was doing."

The Route Of Service

We can believe in what we are doing and feel a permanent sense of fulfillment only if we know we are rendering a service to others. Any undertaking divorced from this feature has no lasting attraction. Never forget that service is the only rent we pay for the space we occupy while we are here on earth.

A person who desires to become rich should certainly not be criticized, provided he desires to become rich for the proper reason. There is nothing wrong with a desire to prosper. We can do so much more for our loved ones and contribute so much more to worthwhile programs in life if we are financially able. But if you are to be successful in such an undertaking, you must never lose sight of this cardinal principle: you can never become truly rich except by enriching the lives of others; you will never truly prosper unless you bring prosperity to others.

So, in filling out our ticket let's not look for the easy route, but for the one that will make ourselves stronger. Also, it should be an optimistic route and a happy route. Never lose sight of the fact that unless it is a route of service it will lead only up a blind alley. Man is so constituted that he must feel a sense of fulfillment if life is to have any permanent meaning. Some people feel that an undertaking must be monumental and world shaking to offer a challenge. This should not be.

The size of the project is of minor importance—of major importance is the unselfish effort and dedication with which we tackle the job. Remember that any place of duty, however small, is a shrine wherein we can glorify our lives with the blessings of service.

Fourth—Are We Willing To Pay The Price?

And finally, at the bottom of any ticket is—the price. So many want to take the trip, but how few are willing to pay the price of the ticket. All of us want to improve our circumstances but how few of us are willing to make the sacrifices to improve ourselves. I get enthusiastic over the idea of building a greater future but do I have that same enthusiasm for the slow tedious task of building myself?

I was attending a college in Greenville, South Carolina, called Furman University. A professor by the name of F.P. Gaines taught me English my freshman year. He later became president of Washington and Lee University.

Dr. Gaines called on us in alphabetical order. I can repeat the entire roll call even to this day. It was important to commit the roster to memory because if you always knew just when you would be called on, there was no need to prepare for recitation except about once every two months—at least that was my feeling during those green years of my life.

Furthermore, good sportsmanship demanded that if a person was sick or absent for any other reason, he was duty bound to protect those students whose names followed his by notifying them in ample time to fortify themselves for recitation.

On a certain day, when my name was fairly well up the list, a very embarrassing situation presented itself. Raleigh and Riley didn't show up at class and neither one had pressed the panic button. I was unprepared, a rather normal condition under the circumstances. I had been over to a neighboring girls' college the night before to see the girl who is now the mother of my five kids.

Fortunately, Dr. Gaines, as he so often did, had departed

from the subject of the day and was giving one of his little informal talks on some phase of personal development. I have long ago forgotten the definition of a nominative predicate or the subjunctive mood. But I shall never forget some of the great inspirational ideas of life he gave us, nor will any who attended his classes ever cease to feel forever the impact of his great personality.

On this particular day, Dr. Gaines had been discussing character. Finally he picked up his roster and I knew that I was to be called on next. I glanced up at the clock and suddenly realized that the dismissal bell would ring in five minutes.

Frantically, as I grabbed a pen and looked for a piece of paper, I blurted out,"Dr. Gaines, could you give us a definition of character that we could write down?"

He looked at me and then up at the clock. I realized how transparent my improvised scheme had turned out to be. But he was the essence of kindness and gentleness. He looked at me and smiled. He realized, of course, that I couldn't have cared less about the definition of character.

Dr. Gaines walked around the room in silence for about a minute with his hands behind him and his chin tilted slightly upward, which was a favorite pose of his. Finally he stopped in front of me, put his left hand on my shoulder and pointed his finger in my face.

"Young fellow," he said, "I'm not sure, but I'm going to give you a definition that I want you to keep until you can find a better one." It was many years ago and I have never heard one half as good. "Character," he said slowly, "Is the ability to carry out a good resolution long after the mood in which it was made has left you." He continued, "Now I didn't say just the ability to carry out a good resolution. We all have our moments of supreme dedication — whether it be fidelity to a person or loyalty to an ideal. But how few of us carry out that resolution when the mood has left us and the tides of temptation come sweeping in."

"Tomorrow morning you are going to have a test on the material we have covered over the past few days. Tonight you will perhaps decide that you are going to get up at six o'clock in the morning and study for this test. And actually you *are* going to get up in the morning—that is, tonight you are, because you are in the mood. But tomorrow morning when you stick your foot out and it touches the cold floor, you don't have that mood any longer. I say character is that which causes you to exercise the self-discipline to get up anyway."

The bell had rung but none of us had heard it. We knew it must have rung because the room was invaded by the next class. Those five minutes have burned brightly for me over the years. I would not exchange them for an entire semester of my college career.

Since that time I've committed myself to a project or assignment many times while I was in an enthusiastic mood. After the mood was gone, the picture was different. The task seemed drab and difficult and without glamor or attraction. The price to pay seemed too high. On such occasions I have tried to remember this definition of character—that which we have within us to substitute for the mood after it is gone.

It's so easy to accept all parts of the ticket except the price. This is where real character and self-discipline enter the picture.

Don't Settle For a Limited Trip

Let's look at our ticket again. If we have a definite destination, if we are wiling to start now, if we don't look for the easy route but for one that will make us stronger, an optimistic route, a route of service and finally, if we are willing to pay the price, then we can, with certainty, know that our little ticket can take us anywhere in life we want to go. I repeat. It can be a magic carpet that will take us to the great city of our dreams, our ambitions and our aspirations. Yes, it can be a key that will open the door to the miracle of life with its limitless possibilities.

This journey is certainly not an easy trip. It's not for little people with little minds. It's not for people who are afraid the sun won't rise tomorrow. It belongs only to those brave and courageous people who dare to dream, have faith and expect the best. If you really want to take the trip, you must be willing to be baptized by immersion in some of the tougher aspects of life.

It was about 2,000 years ago that a great Greek philosopher and mathematician, Archimedes, was asked if he could perform a certain task.

This is what he said, "Give me a lever that is long enough, give me a fulcrum that is strong enough and give me a place to stand and single-handed I will move the world."

Our lever is our goal in life. Our fulcrum is our self-discipline and willingness to pay the price. Furthermore, we must stand upon the firm ground of dedication and belief in our pursuits and activities in this life. If we have these qualities, we too can move the world.

Read and re-read this chapter, over and over. It has tools of greatness you can't afford to ignore. Practice its principles and resolve to start your trip today.

8

O-KYAK-A-SAN

Murray Raphael
Gordon's Alley
Atlantic City, NJ 08401
609/348-6646

A recent article in USA Today said, "Investing in business isn't a sure thing. In fact, business failures this year aren't expected to drop substantially from the 1983 post-depression record of 31,334."

They didn't. In fact more businesses failed this past year including the largest number of bank failures since the depression.

Yes, there was also a record-breaking number of NEW businesses opening but the question I ask is, "How can I make sure I'm not listed in the obituary pages of the Business Section of the newspaper next year? What am I doing to make sure I don't have to take down my neon, fold my tent and silently move away?"

You might easily feel you are in a crisis situation.

The Chinese wrote the word "crisis" nearly 3,400 years ago. It looks like this:

Now, if you take the character on the left, all by itself, it means "danger." I'm in a dangerous situation.

But if you take the character on the right, all by itself, it means "opportunity."

The Chinese word for crisis has two characters — and one of them stands for opportunity.

If I'm having a tough time in my business, the competition is as well. Here's one reason why: the consumer identifies all businesses as "alike."

All supermarkets sell food. All clothing stores sell clothing. All banks sell financial products and services. What are you doing that's different, special and in front of your competition?

Here's one simple, positive, always-works rule: take care of your customers.

In our seminars around the world we tell our audiences, "'Tis far, far easier to sell more to the customer you have than to sell a new customer." Yet in a recent survey on Why Customers Leave You, the answers were as follows:

Nine percent were lured away by other stores.

Nine percent moved.

Fourteen percent had complaints that were not taken care of.

Sixty eight percent left for no particular reason.

In other words, nearly seven out of 10 customers leave your business because you let them leave.

What do the Japanese do to keep customers?

When you enter a store in Japan, you will find several people on either side of the entrance. They bow down and greet you as you walk in and they say, "O-Kyak-a-san." That translates to "You are a visitor to our home."

Do customers feel that way when they walk into YOUR business? Do they feel as though you invited them over to talk, be comfortable, feel "at home?" Or do they feel like they are strangers?

Stanley Marcus, whose family founded the Neiman Marcus department store, wrote a great book called *Minding the Store*. It has excellent philosophy for anyone in business and one sentence in the book summed it up best. "My father said," he wrote, "that our business is a member of our family."

As soon as I read that I knew what he meant! Many in business today were around at the birth and watched it grow and suffered the anxiety you suffer with any newborn. And soon it achieved its own identity and you shared the pride because when customers came into your business they were dealing with a "member of your family," they were "a visitor to your home."

At a recent convention in Atlantic City, New Jersey, Lee Iacocca, Chrysler's chairman, addressed 5,000 Dodge dealers showing them the new year's models. He walked in, stood behind the podium and 5,000 Dodge dealers stood up and gave him a standing ovation before he even said a word. Why not? Most of them in the room would not be in business if it were not for him.

He spoke for about 45 minutes about the new cars and then he closed his speech saying, "Every year at these meetings I tell you how to do more business in your agency. Tonight I'm going to give you the secret and it's only four words.

"I'm not going to talk about the Japanese automobile imports and how they are hurting our business."

"I'm not going to deny tonight that I'm running for the presidency of the United States."

"What I am going to do is to show you how to do more business next year. It's only four words. Here they are: **MAKE SOMEONE LIKE YOU**."

"You see," he said, "all automobile dealers are alike — they all sell automobiles."

"You see, the customers can go to any dealer and get any color they want."

"You see, the customer can go to any dealer and get any add on accessory they want."

"But, if you **MAKE SOMEONE LIKE YOU**, they will tell three other customers and they will tell six and they will tell 20 and pretty soon you're going to have to employ more sales people and get guards to handle the crowds at the door."

"Listen, you want to do more business next year? It's easy. **MAKE SOMEONE LIKE YOU!**"

I wanted to stand and cheer and shout. Isn't that what it's all about? Making someone feel they are the most important person that comes into your business for a very simple reason: THEY ARE!

We were in a men's clothing store a few months ago and I went up to the owner and said, "Michael, your store is really busy."

"Ah, yes," he answered proudly, "That's 'cause we have a lot of customers."

"What's that mean?" we asked.

"It means," he said, "that we're busy because we have a lot of customers."

"But Michael," we said, "having a customer is only HALF WAY up the Loyalty Ladder. What you want to do is have them all the way up at the top."

"What's THAT mean?" he asked.

We explained.

The bottom rung of the latter is Suspects.

SUSPECTS are your total universe of EVERYONE who could possibly buy your goods or services.

Too large a group to work. Too expensive in terms of time, advertising, marketing. You have to concentrate on a narrower group which is the next step up the ladder. They are Prospects.

PROSPECTS are people who have heard about you but still have not shopped with you. They have seen your name in advertising or know about you from a friend or neighbor. The first time they come in and shop with you they become a customer.

CUSTOMERS are people that have spent one dollar with you one time. But they could also be a customer of your competition as well. They know about you but are not committed to you. We have to bring them to the next step of the ladder and have them be a Client.

CLIENTS are people who buy everything you have to sell that they can possibly use.

How do you have them do that? One way: Practice the Art of Active Listening. When your customers talk to you are you listening AT them or TO them? One of the quickest ways to succeed (or fail) in business is to listen (or NOT listen) to your customers.

Let's take a pause right here to give you the SECRET RULE OF SELLING. It's only one sentence. Memorize it and you'll never have to attend another selling seminar the rest of your life. Here is the Secret Rule of Selling:

Find out what the customers want to buy . . . and give it to them.

That's it. If you are a supermarket owner and you stock avocados and the customers don't buy avocados, are you still going to stock them as heavily? If you own a clothing store and all you wear are oxford button down shirts but your customers like plain spread collars, which are you going to buy?

Right. Listening to your customers enables them to become . . . Clients.

Stew Leonard has a supermarket in Norwalk, Connecticut. You can see his name in the next edition of the Guiness Book of World Records for doing more business per square foot than any store of any kind in the world!

More than 100,000 customers go through his store EVERY WEEK spending more than a hundred million dollars a year!

But aren't all supermarkets alike? Don't they all sell food?

Not this one. Well, yes, they sell food but look what happens when you walk into the front door of the store. There is a 6,000 pound rock greeting you. Carved out of the rock at the top is this phrase: "Our Policy." And then carved directly below it is this:

Rule #1: The customer is always right.

Rule #2: If the customer is wrong, re-read rule #1.

He has a Suggestion Box which has more than 100 suggestions from customers every day. Stew makes sure the customer is written to or called THE SAME DAY to answer their question, complaint or suggestion.

He walks through the store constantly asking customers, "What do you like? What don't you like?" He runs focus group sessions with customers to find out what they want him to have in his store.

When you realize that average supermarket customers will spend nearly a quarter of a million dollars in their lifetime, you understand why Stew Leonard cares about his customers — makes sure they feel like they are a "visitor to his home."

Come with me and let's visit Tom and Hayden Edwards in Madisonville, Kentucky. Madisonville, Kentucky has a population of 17,000 and about 15 supermarkets. Yet Tom and Hayden do more business in THEIR supermarket than the next three supermarkets put together!

What do they do that's different?

This: When you're checking out of the store, Tom or Hayden are usually there asking, "Was everything O.K.? Did you find everything you wanted?"

And if you answered, "Gee Tom, we couldn't find any Durkee pepper." He'll turn to one of the bagging boys and say, "Charlie, please get some Durkee pepper for these folks." And when Charlie comes back are we impressed? Would you be?

Or perhaps Charlie comes back and says, "Tom, we're out of Durkee pepper."

Tom hands you a slip of paper and says, "Would you put your name and telephone number here and the item you want and I'll call you when it comes in."

AND HE DOES!

He practices a little known rule of selling called DWYPYWD which, translated, means, "Do What You Promised You Would Do."

Most people do not.

Listen to this statistic: 90% of Americans do not associate the word 'trust' with the word 'business.'

Now go back and read that last paragraph one more time.

What happens if the American consumer finds a store they can trust?

A recent survey of shoppers all over the U.S. asked the question, "What do you want most from the store or business where you shop or buy?"

Their number one answer: (No, folks, not price) was; CONFIDENCE!

People want to feel comfortable, taken care of . . . a "visitor to your home."

If that's true (and it is) then your customer has become a Client.

But there's still one more rung of the ladder to climb.

How can that be? If a customer is buying everything from you they can possibly use, how can there still be a higher rung of Loyalty?

There is. It's called an Advocate.

An ADVOCATE is someone who tells the rest of the world they must, should, have to shop with you.

Someone moves into town and says, "Where should I buy my groceries?" Do you say, "All supermarkets are alike?" (or "All banks are alike? Or all clothing stores are alike." Or . . .). NO. You take them by the hand and bring them down to the nearest supermarket where YOU shop. You introduce them to the manager. You tell the manager the name of the people and you want them treated the same way he treats YOU.

That's what an Advocate is . . . someone who runs all around town making sure everyone does business with you.

We want to have all of our customers climb to the top of the Loyalty Ladder.

And we do that by caring about them, by taking care of them, by worrying over them. By doing everything in a First Class manner.

That's what Walt Disney did.

He left Kansas City, Missouri, in 1926 after he had gone bankrupt. Took baby pictures to raise enough money for the train ticket to Hollywood where he wanted to work in animation.

Sold the pictures but didn't have enough money for the ticket he wanted so he sold the camera. And he boarded the train in Kansas City, Missouri, with a plaid sport jacket, mis-matched plaid pants and a cardboard suitcase with three changes of underwear and went to Los Angeles, California, on the train . . . FIRST CLASS!

"I wanted to arrive First Class," he said, "because that's the only way I knew to do things."

And when you visit Disneyland or Disney World you will see his philosophy at work. You will feel as though you are a "visitor to his home."

When Epcot in Disney World opened, CBS brought Eric Severied out of retirement to host a TV special. And Severied said that Walt Disney was a genius who said the world was divided into three groups of people: The Well Poisoners, the Lawn Mowers and the Life Enhancers.

The Well Poisoners are the ones who tell you the reasons why things can't be done. One of our favorite expressions is, "Cut out the complaints and most people have nothing to say." Listen to people talk. They complain about weather. And politics. And business. Listen and then say, "Uh, what do you want ME to do about that?" And they will look at you kind of odd and walk out. And that's fine . . .

The Lawn Mowers are the ones who say, "We've been doing it this way in our business the same way for the past 25 years, so why should we change? We'll just keep on mowing the lawn in the same direction in the same manner. Every year. Never change.

The Life Enhancers are the ones that wake up in the morning and say, "What can I do today to make somebody else's life a little better?

The next time you hear someone say to you, "I'm a self-made man" or "I'm a self-made woman," don't believe it. It's not true. There was SOMEONE—a mother, a father, a grandparent, a friend, a someone . . . who opened the door for them one time and said, "Come on in."

And once you cross the threshold, you have an obligation to help someone else.

There's a good book by David Duncan called, *Try Giving Yourself Away*. He lists different ideas for you to do every day to make someone else's life a little more enjoyable: Standing in a line, let the person behind you go first. Parking a car, let someone else have the space.

And so the next time you go into your work or business and it's early in the morning, and there's no one there, and you're in a place that in a few minutes will be busy with staff and customers and everyone running around absorbed with their personal needs and worries and thoughts, stop for a moment. Look around. And then softly say to yourself . . .

"Starting today . . . I'm going to be . . . a Life Enhancer!"

9

A PSYCHOLOGIST'S PERSPECTIVE ON EXCELLENCE

Herb True
1717 E. Colfax
South Bend, IN 46617
219/234-2340

One statement that can be made about everybody everywhere is that we're different weights. We can say that people have different I.Q.s. We can say that people are different heights, but, the one statement that we can make about everybody is . . .no one has reached his potential.

Human potential is the least understood and the most squandered source on the face of this earth. Let's take women . . .we've squandered tremendous female talent when we really could learn so much from women. For example, what is man's best friend? A dog. What's woman's best friend? Diamonds. Have you ever tried to hock a dog?

What can we do to increase the quality of our performance? How can we get closer to reaching our potential? Think of your performance not as a square, not as a triangle, but as a circle. Think of half of that circle being your desire and half being your capability. So half your performance is desire and half of your performance is capability. It's one's desire times his capability that gives him his performance.

Your desire is influenced by your environment. Suppose your friends call and invite you to play a game of golf. If it's a beautiful day, you may feel a strong desire to go play. However, if it's raining, you may not wish to go. Your desire is a combination of the environment multiplied by your attitude toward that environment.

I grew up in Oklahoma where I was poor and had no toys. I used to slide down the hill on my cousin. I look at my kids and they've got their own environment. They have their own hi-fi stereo and ten speed bike. If they wanted to run away from home they would have to call Mayflower van lines. They've got their own bedrooms and their own beds. Since I had two brothers, I never had either my own room or my own bed. I never even slept alone, until I got married.

What is the environment in the U.S.? We have a dictator and we call it "change." Think about it, that's our dictator. If there is magic in being a human being, the magic is the sensitivity to recognize that moment in passing—that little increment of time just before what you're doing is old and obsolete and the new becomes necessary for survival.

Take, for example, the change in our approach to women. Look at the research. We're finding all kinds of exciting things that women can do better.

What are we finding out about Chicanos? By the year 2000, more people in the U.S. will speak Spanish than speak English.

To talk about change means talking about forecasting. What's going to happen in the 21st century? There are people who forecast and then there are people who like *Megatrends* say, "It's already happening."

We've already changed from an industrial society to an information society. We've already changed from a hierarchy where we have an organization chart with one man at the top who walks around saying, "I am the boss, just think of me as a friend who is always right." Now we're finding out there are different kinds of organizational charts that are more like a wheel. They're called networks. In the 1960's the big concern was discrimination against the blacks. In the 70's we almost forgot about the blacks because we were concerned about discrimination against women. Now, it's the 1980's. In the 1990's we will have discrimination against older people.

My mentor is Bill Gove. We have done rally work together. Bill Gove is thirteen years older than I am — biologically and chronologically. But in terms of his dreams, in terms of his hopes and in terms of his ability to give, he is the youngest, most playful man you'll ever know.

So what is success? What is excellence? You can read at a thousand words a minute, but you can't think at a thousand words a minute. How fast can you feel? Is it best to do a thousand things one percent better, or, to do one thing a thousand times better? The most successful organizations have a reputation for doing the little things well. Excellence is made up of a thousand little things all being done well.

You're in the business to make a profit. The customer's the boss, and you're in business to serve the customer's need. If you don't serve that customer's need, you'll be like the guy who started a tall man shop in Tokyo. You ain't gonna make it, man. You may sell lots of suits and lots of clothes, but you're going to lose it on alterations. Nobody is immune to this.

The people who are excellent are continually asking me, "What's the big need?" How do we meet other people's needs? I would say consider the customer to be the boss. Also, remember that environment is a variable over which you have no control — it changes. And if your performance, if your excellence is going to be better or worse, it's affected one way or another by something we call attitude.

Your desire is a combination of your attitude multiplied by the environment. The most powerful force that you and I have is what we tell ourselves and believe. I believe in positive thinking; it's the positive talkers that bug me. If you read the book on positive thinking, you probably realize the key word is thinking, not positive. I see a lot of positive....I play golf with a positive talker. He's gonna drive this water hole. He didn't drive it last year, but he's gonna do it this time. So he gets some new boots and some new clubs. But he gets up there and he puts down an old ball. He's going to do it with old ideas and old attitudes.

I am judged on the number of times that I succeed; I'm not judged on the number of times I fail. And the number of times I succeed is in direct proportion to the number of times I can fail and keep on trying. What do I tell myself? I made a mistake. I made a big mistake but did I fail? No, I made a mistake. Many people succeed when nobody else believes in them, but never does a person succeed when they don't believe in themselves.

I have a 118 IQ. You can't even get into Notre Dame with a 118 IQ, but you can teach there. I was told in grade school and in high school that I was dumb. I can show you at the top of my college transcript 15 hours of F. Then I went into the Marine Corps. I found out that I'm not dumb, I'm different. I learn fast, but I forget quick. Then I earned a bachelors degree from the University of Oklahoma. I took all those tough courses like oral penmanship. I married in my junior year of college and we had a child the same month my wife and I graduated. We had two children. My point in bringing this up is that I've been blessed. I've had great teachers.

My mother is 88. Her recall is down to about fifteen minutes but she still teaches. My new teachers are my own children and my daughters-in-law. Since the beginning of time, before we even knew about the right brain or the left brain, the sages of the ages said, "You do not control your thoughts but you can influence your thoughts."

It always terrifies me when I see pornography. When I was a kid we didn't have as much pornography. It wasn't slicked up and made to look like something really great. People are brilliant; they don't eat rancid food. Why? Because it makes you sick. Aren't there things that you can put in your head that can make you sicker than anything you can put in your belly? Watch your thoughts; they become your words.

Say words enough, program them in there, and the right brain picks them up. Your words become your actions and your actions become your habits. In working with young adults, I try to explain child abuse to them. Every parent who has ever beaten a child learned to beat children, but you can choose to change. So I explain to young gals that if they want to know what a guy is going to be like before they marry him, they should go to his home. Go see how his father treats him. A young man can change, but you should know what he's been taught. One girl said, "I don't have time for that. When I get serious about someone I just explain to him that there will be no pushing around. Three hundred and sixty-five days after you hit me the first time, you will have been dead a year."

The death and the life of the environment is your reaction to it. It's your attitude times your environment that gives you your desires. What's the other part? How capable are you? Your capability is a combination of your knowledge times your skill. When someone says they want to earn more money, they want to earn more love or they want to earn more respect, one letter can change it. Just write down To Earn More, and the answer is Learn More. Maybe you can learn more about yourself, about your environment and about your competition.

The area of knowledge is overwhelming. What makes a difference in psychology and many pseudo sciences is that we don't really have many ideas, so we keep renaming the old ones. That's great. What is it that makes a difference? I don't know how many times I've seen this, but I try to say to myself when I meet somebody, "People want to know how much you care before they care how much you know."

I know how to kill so beautifully but do I know how to create? One day I killed my son's joy in the victory of his team by complaining about his dirty clothes ripped at the seams. The day before, I killed my daughter's pride in the dress she made by pointing out every fault, then adding my faint praise. One day I killed a friendship and turned affection into hate. I misunderstood, but I said it too late. I've killed my spouse's love, not with a mighty blow, but bit by bit, year by year.

"Where have you been?" "I've been to the beauty parlor." "What's the matter, was it closed?" I find myself saying things in a tone and in a manner to my wife I wouldn't say to a clerk at the Hutson's.

People want to know how much you care. God does not expect great things from me. He expects love from me, because I've had love. Expecting some people to love is expecting too much. They certainly can give. I can't give piano lessons; I can give forgiveness. It ain't tough for me, I've been forgiven. Bishop Sheen spoke at the prison in Minnesota. He went in and his first words were, "We have so much in common. We've all sinned, but you've been caught."

I kill or I create. What am I going to give? Am I going to give joy? Am I going to give hope? What are the options that I have?

Let's go back to knowledge. There are things in knowledge I have that I don't like, I don't want it to be true. I wish I could change it. We now know that there is empirical evidence that people make decisions about other people based upon what the person is wearing. We make decisions about other people based on their grooming. We make big decisions about their economic level and their trustworthiness just by what they wear. Go into a store. Wear old jeans, wear worn out tennis shoes, wear an old Marine jacket and nobody even wants to see you. Dress up and even the customers come to see you. I wish it weren't that way.

So in this great technological world what kind of knowledge could I give you that I would want you to remember more than anything else? Something I want to remember myself. The hardest lesson I have to learn is the affect that I do have on other people. They call it bank balance. If I give somebody respect, esteem, the time of day, I'm making a deposit in the bank. If I give them a quick shuffle or a little twist, I'm making a withdrawal.

I have children in whose bank I am overdrawn. We got one son that's for sale. He ain't a bad kid. He went to college and he did poorly. Couldn't make that 8 o'clock class — and he was going to night school! He was studying hard, but he was highlighting his book with a black magic marker.

The first stage of life is Leave Me Alone. That comes at about 14. Anybody who has 12, 13 or 14 year old kids know that it's Leave Me Alone time! That stage lasts for some people till they are 50. We have 50 year old people saying, "Leave me alone. I don't need any damn help."

The second stage of life, with your children and maybe with you, is at 25 when they say, "Help me." You know this type if you have kids 25....this is a kid who wants help with the insurance on his car or buying a home.

Then at about 35 this marvelous thing happens. The fourth stage of life is Let Me Help You. This is a trap for some fathers. "I've got to help my daughter. I've got to give her a better car because I can't have her driving that kind of car." "Now wait a minute Dad. I don't want a better car. I bought that car. You want to do something with that money? Buy a microwave oven for Mom." The fourth stage is awkward. "I Don't Have To Help You, But If You Ever Want Or Need Help, Call Me." I warn you that if you say this to anybody and you really mean it, they're gonna call you. They're gonna catch that feeling. As Marilyn Monroe said, "I can't just learn the words. I have to learn the feelings." If they ever feel that, they'll call you. But, I warn you it will be the most inopportune moment of your life.

What about all of these skills that we have—the management skills, the marketing skills, the finance skills, the human skills, the entrepreneurial skills, all these skills? Why is the listening skill so important? If you go to managers, why do they charge you $150 an hour to listen?

The planning skill is also important. The will to win isn't everything, but the will to prepare to win is. If you listen to the excellent things you will find over and over the requirement of having a plan. I want to give you only one area of the plan. What are your priorities? I have Jewish friends whose number one priority is to Give Thee Our Father before they get out of bed. I have teachers whose number one priority is to touch every student. Our families should be a top priority.

Mr. McKay of the Mormon church says, "No other success can compensate for failure at home." Notice the critical word there is failure. We all make mistakes. Marriage is the only war in which you sleep with the enemy. My wife and I married for better or worse. I couldn't do any better and she couldn't do any worse.

What have we said? Number one, don't let the environment turn you off. Say, "That really turns me on. I see some opportunity there that I wouldn't see anywhere else." Your life has a special purpose regardless of what the environment is. You were not an accident. You may have been a surprise to your parents, but you're not an accident. You'd be impossible to replace, and there will never be another you.

We all have to make very difficult decisions in life. Art Holst said, "You make a decision, it's gonna be good, or bad, or happy or sad." Immanuel Kant said, "You make the difference." He also said, "To be is to do." Sigmund Freud said, "To do is to be." And Frank Sinatra said, "Do be do be do."

Lord, I ain't what I ought to be. With my potential I ought to be more loving and more open. I ain't what I want to be. I want to be more sensitive; I want to be more patient and more tolerant. Lord, I ain't what I'm gonna be. Thank you, Lord. I ain't what I used to be.

10

KEEPING GOOD CUSTOMERS— THE GRANDMA FACTOR

Jim Cathcart
P.O. Box 9075
La Jolla, CA 92038
619/459-1515
800/222-4883

In 1975 I moved from Little Rock, Arkansas, to Tulsa, Oklahoma, to take advantage of a new job opportunity. I had a habit at that time of eating the same breakfast every morning at a particular fast food restaurant.

Well, when I moved to Tulsa it broke up my routine. So I decided that the best thing I could do would be to find one of those same fast food chains at which to get my breakfast. I went looking through my neighborhood and, luckily, about one mile from the office, I found the place. I drove in, parked my car and walked up to the counter where two young ladies stood. One woman was about 27 years old and the other was in her very early 20's. I spoke to the older of the two women.

We exchanged greetings and she said, "What will you

have?" I ordered an egg sandwich and coffee and she took my order and asked my name. That was the first time that anyone in a fast food restaurant had ever asked me my name.

I said, "My name is Jim Cathcart, now that you're interested."

"Well, Mr. Cathcart," she said, "breakfast is coming right up and that'll be a $1.41."

I said, "Well, terrific. Thank you."

About that time the younger of the two women said, "Hey, Grandma, where are those coffee cups?"

I said, "Grandma? You don't look old enough to be a grandma to me."

"No," she said, "I'm not a grandma. But, I am sort of the mother hen around here, so they call me Grandma."

I said, "Well, what do you like to be called?"

"If I had my own choice I'd rather be called by my own name, Marilyn."

I said, "Marilyn, thank you very much. I'll enjoy my breakfast and I'll see you later."

I went back, sat down and ate my breakfast. I came back the next day, walked in and Marilyn said, "Good morning. Now, what is your name again?"

I said, "Cathcart. Jim Cathcart."

"Good morning, Mr. Cathcart, what will you have?"

I said, "I'll have an egg sandwich and coffee."

"Terrific," she said, "That'll be $1.41." Somehow there was a pattern emerging here.

I got my breakfast, went back and sat down. I was pleased that she had taken an interest in me, but it was no big deal. I went on about my business, and every few days I'd go back by there, walk in and order the same thing. After a while she'd say, "Good morning, Mr. Cathcart."

One morning she said, "Good morning, Mr. Cathcart. Your breakfast is ready."

I said, "How did you know what I was going to have?"

She said, "Trust me, Mac, you're predictable."

I said, "I'll bet it's a $1.41."

She said, "Okay, okay. I'm predictable too." So I paid my $1.41 and had my breakfast.

About four months passed before I went back. As I was driving into the parking lot, I noticed two very large buses. Ninety bodies were in that lobby, packed like sardines, standing in line to get their breakfast.

I thought. "This is a good day to go have pancakes." Then I thought, "No wait a minute. This is my place; I feel at home here. I'm going to go have my egg sandwich." So I walked up, opened the door and squeezed in among all those people.

I got in and looked for the line that was moving fastest, the one that always stops once you get in it. I got in that line, and sure enough, it stopped. So I resigned myself to being in line for another twenty or thirty minutes.

Shortly I heard, "Mr. Cathcart."

I looked around wondering where the voice was coming from.

"Mr. Cathcart." I looked between the lines and down there at the counter was Grandma. She said, "Mr. Cathcart, your breakfast is ready."

I said as I walked forward, "My breakfast is ready. Excuse me, pardon me."

I worked my way through the crowd, ready to lay out my $1.41, when she said, "Oh no. It's on the house."

I picked up the tray. I really felt very important. The other people were saying, "Who's this guy? Is he the owner or the Regional Vice-President?

With that little gesture, Grandma, or Marilyn as she preferred to be called, bought about seven years of loyalty from me. I came back every morning I could. I brought business associates. We had business meetings there, and you don't typically have business meetings in that sort of a place.

Let's go back and examine what took place. Put yourself in the position of Grandma. How hard would it be with one customer, just one customer, to learn his or her name and remember it? Not very hard. I'm not suggesting that you have to memorize the name of every customer, I'm just saying if you can memorize one, it might do you some good. How much did it cost her to give me a complimentary breakfast that morning? A lot of people say it cost her a $1.41. In net it probably cost about .02 cents. But, regardless what the net cost was, let's say it cost her a $1.41. Do you think it was a wise investment on her part? Sure it was.

There are a couple of problems though. How can you tell your employees, "I want you to give away the store. Find a guy, learn his name, and give him free food." You can't afford to give gifts to your customers all the time.

But let's look at the situation a little more closely. When I walked in, the place was packed. She had noticed out of the corner of her eye that I had driven into the parking lot. She recognized my car because I had been coming there for quite some time. When she saw that car she knew that it meant egg sandwich and coffee, $1.41. So she saw the car, looked at this mob of people in front of her and thought, "Gee, there's no way I can maintain their good will and let this guy come from the back all the way to the front. What I'll do is give him a free breakfast. It won't interrupt my work flow; he'll feel very special; I'll feel good that I did the right thing, and everybody else will be wondering what in the world is going on, but I won't lose any good will."

So she called me forward as she was filling someone else's order; set mine there, set theirs there and said, "Mr. Cathcart, your breakfast is ready." I got my breakfast and I was a happy man.

See, whenever a customer goes into your organization, and buys something, whether it happens to be one little tiny item or a large service, he has, in effect, paid his membership dues — just like joining a club. A customer is like a member of a club — a special organization they have joined by paying whatever dues are required.

Usually you expect two things from your membership. You expect to be recognized — you're a member. You expect that they will identify you as one of them instead of one of those people out there. Also, you expect special treatment.

In this case, I got recognition, and I loved to go to breakfast there. I brought my business associates and they'd say, "You're going there for breakfast?" I'd say, "We are going there for breakfast." We'd walk into the place and she'd always say, "Good morning, Mr. Cathcart. Your breakfast is ready." My friend would walk up and order breakfast and get courtesy but no special treatment.

It was obvious I was the special guy in the group. That's the feeling she gave me. She went out of her way to make me feel special — to give me that little extra touch, that little extra special treatment. One sincere act like that, one sincere gesture from one of your people in your organization can buy you years of loyalty that you couldn't get with the most expensive promotional campaign on earth. One little simple thing.

There's an old adage that was used many years ago. It's still used today and I think it's very similar to what we're talking about. "To have a friend, be a friend." In business "to have a customer, be a friend." Don't just look at building a customer base or client base. Look at building business friendships. That's when the people move from customer to client and they come back all the time.

You may feel that what I'm really saying is that we need more professionalism, and it's true that we do. But we need to bear in mind one simple fact — a profession, these days, is not determined by the business you're in, it's determined by the way you're in business. A professional recognizes that he or she must concentrate not on additional effort but on additional effectiveness.

Effectiveness is a combination of three things. Think of it as a triangle. The first thing is the technical knowledge and skills that you have, what you academically understand and know and have learned about your business. The second thing is interpersonal skills. In other words, your ability to relate your ideas in different ways to different people. And the third thing, the final edge of that triangle, is self-management skills. The technical knowledge and skills would be the base of the triangle. That's the foundation of what makes you effective. If you didn't have the basic skills, the basic technical knowledge in your field, you'd have to get into another business. You'd have to choose another field or start over from scratch. You have to have that, but, that's not the thing that determines whether you really do well or just get by.

The Carnegie foundation did a study many years ago. The results of that study have been widely broadcast. They studied a variety of professions — law, medicine, retail sales, manufacturing, management, all sorts of things — trying to determine what contributes the most to a person's long-term, over-all career success.

They found that only 15% of success comes from how technically competent you are. Eighty-five percent of your success comes from a combination of your ability to deal with people and your ability to manage yourself.

One way to define self-management is being able to get yourself to do what needs to be done when it needs to be done whether you feel like it or not and still do a decent job of it. That's self management. I think that, coupled with the ability to deal effectively with people, is what's going to truly determine whether you're just moderately successful or fantastically successful in your chosen field.

Someone said one time "Wait a minute, Cathcart. I don't want any doctors operating on me with 15% technical competence." I sure don't blame them, I don't either. But, it's not that they would only have 15% technical competence, it's just that their technical competence only contributes about 15% to their over all achievement level in their field, doctor, lawyer, merchant or whatever. So, when we look at it that way, we can see that it is vitally important that we have a whole lot more going for us than just a good education. Remember the words we used to hear so often? "If you want to be a success, you've got to get a good education." We found that there are a lot of well-educated, totally unsuccessful people out there. So there is much more to it than just that.

Look at the market place, at all the businesses out there and the people in the same basic field that you're involved in. You'll find that the products and services available from you and the products available from others are not all that different. Certainly you have some unique qualities that help you stand apart. But, in the general market place, there are a lot of other people, regardless of your field, that do generally the kind of thing you do. There are a lot of other people whose price is not that much different from yours. When there is not much difference in the product and there's not much difference in the price, there'd better be a great big difference in the way you deal with people.

That's the message I want to convey to you. We look at who we're dealing with and how we're dealing with them. Think in terms of building a business friendship. That's the key.

There was a man in Europe about a year and a half ago who was trying to find an American firm that could do some consulting work for him. He wanted sales and management training. He studied several firms. He chose what he thought were the top ones and he went to visit those people. My name happened to fall into the hat. He went to the others first and then he came to La Jolla, California, where our offices are today.

He walked into the office and met with me for two or three hours. I gave him a short tour of the community and sent him on his way. He hired me and we have now been to Europe three times during the elapsed time between that initial interview and now. We've built a very solid, very valuable client relationship. We've been able to help a great deal and we've been able to build some friendships that go along with that, so it's a very nice experience.

The last time I was there I sat down with him in Brussels, propped my feet up, and said, "Tell me something. Why did you choose us?" He said, "Jim, I interviewed a lot of people, a lot of firms and the other firms were impressive. They had the credentials; they had the beautiful printed material; they had the classy looking offices, they had all the things that you would want to have. But something was missing. I came to La Jolla and met you. I talked with the people in your firm. You had a philosophy. It showed in the way you do business and I decided that I wanted my people thinking, believing and behaving like they do in that office in La Jolla. That's why I hired you."

We've got to practice what we preach. We've got to be able to express in the way we do our business the practical day to day application of the philosophies we espouse — the things that we claim to agree with and believe in.

The Grandma factor, which is what I'm fond of calling this, is something that we have to decide on our own to consciously cultivate. I'd like you to ask yourself this question. What is the Grandma factor in your business? Think about it. How many of your own people in your organization, or the organization that you are affiliated with, practice the kind of orientation toward the customer-thinking of that person as a potential friend that we saw in Grandma?

How many of them think in terms of building business relationships that will endure over time instead of merely being profitable for right now, for today? We've got a real obligation, not only to do that ourselves, but to make it contagious and get our people catching this attitude, or this way of operating. We've got to, as some people say, lead by example.

But, I've got news for you friends. You can't *not* lead by example. Did you ever consider that? It is totally impossible not to lead by example. Everything you do, every time you go out there to try and create some kind of result, you're setting an example and someone else is watching you and saying, "I think I'll do it that way," or "If she can get by with it I can get by with it," or "If he's going to do it that way, why don't I? It seems easier his way."

So they're watching us. They're watching the good examples we set, and they're also watching the not so good examples. I think there is a strong obligation on our part to fulfill that in the right way. The poet Edgar Guest expressed this idea very well. What Edgar Guest said was summed up in one poem so perfectly. He said,

"I would rather see a sermon than hear one any day.
I would rather you walk with me than merely show
  the way.
And the lectures you deliver might be very wise and
  true,
but I think I'll get my lesson by observing what you
  do.
Because I might misunderstand you and all this high
  advice you give,
but there is no misunderstanding how you act and
  how you live."

We're always leading by example. If you'll set the example, I'll guarantee you some of the folks will catch that. And what we'll have is a whole society permeated with the Grandma factor.

11

THE CHALLENGE
OF EXCELLENCE

Art Holst
2001 W. Willow Knolls Rd.,
Suite 206
Peoria, IL 61614
309/691-9339

My first year as a line judge in the National Football League was 1964. I was working a game in Cleveland and the fullback was Jim Brown. Six foot two inches and ran the 100 in about 9.5 – tough to bring down. Cleveland was playing Dallas. Brown came through the line with a ball and a big middle line backer for Dallas went to tackle him. When he did he grabbed Brown's face mask. That isn't fair and that's why we're out there. I threw the flag, stopped the clock and told the referee, "I've got number 55 on the defense pulling the face mask! Personal foul! 15 yards!" About that time, this guy jumped up; all 6' 6", 260 pounds of him. He looked down at me and said, "What?" I said, "Get back in there and play football before I bite your head off." They're all real good guys. He very politely said, "If you do, sir, you'll have more brains in your stomach than you have in your head."

So I'm not an expert on any intellectual subject. But when you're out there you're a little like Raquel Welch's elbows, everybody knows they're there, but nobody cares. My last game in the National Football League was in 1979 at the championship game in Pittsburgh in the freezing rain between Pittsburgh and Houston. Four weeks before that I had been in Pittsurgh for a late afternoon, nationally televised game between Pittsburgh and the Dallas Cowboys. The score was 21-17 in favor of Pittsburgh. In the third quarter Roger Staubauch, who was quarterbacking Dallas, got hit in the head and went down.

Now, a time out for an injured player prior to the last two minutes of the half does not count against the three that they guard so carefully; it's a referee's timeout. But, unbeknownst to us the scoreboard operator in Pittsburgh, a guy I'll never meet who probably thinks his job doesn't account for anything, put one time-out up on the board for Dallas when there were really none. We don't look at the scoreboard. We can't even see the scoreboard!

That's one of the criteria for working in this league, if you can see the scoreboard you don't qualify! At least that's what a lot of fans think! So we've got one timeout up on the board for Dallas when there were really none. Staubauch comes back in and two or three plays later he's hit again and down he goes. We signal a time out, still no charged timeouts against Dallas. The scoreboard operator puts "two" up on the scoreboard. Now, with a minute and 50 seconds left to go in the football game, Dallas' ball, on the Pittsburgh 25, Dallas is still down by four points. Staubauch calls his first time out. We mark one on the card and the scoreboard operator puts "three" up on the scoreboard.

Now we have a developing problem in communications. When things are not what they are, they are what? What people think they are! And 55,000 people in Pittsburgh thought there were three time-outs against Dallas. Now with a minute and 20 seconds to go in the ball game, it's Dallas' ball on the Pittsburgh 20. Staubauch called his second time out, Dallas. We marked it down and the scorekeeper put "four" up on the scoreboard! Immediately Chuck Noll, the coach for the Pittsburgh Steelers, began to holler at me,

"Pardon me," or words to that effect. I couldn't figure out what this great coach was so upset about. I didn't even turn around.

With 20 seconds left in the ball game, Dallas' ball on the Pittsburgh 18, fourth down, Staubauch called his third and last time out for Dallas. The scorekeeper puts "five" up on the scoreboard and Chuck Noll hollered out, "Turn around and talk to me you dirty Framisamis Peppaloomer! I turned around and said, "What do you want to talk about coach?" He said, "I want to talk about how many timeouts you're giving Dallas!" Now he was standing in that six-foot wide white stripe he was not supposed to be in. I said, "We're giving them three, and you get back out of the white." The coach said, "You've already given them five!" As he said this he took two steps across the white onto the field right in front of my nose. I said, "No, coach. We've given them three but I'm going to give you 15 yards!"

I threw the flag in the air. Oh, was that popular in Pittsburgh! They were going to name me Steel Queen. Bob Fredric, the referee, had just told Landry that he'd used his last timeout. He turned around just in time to see my yellow rag hit the ground. Fifty-five thousand people started to boo me. He ran all the way across the field and said, "Artie, what have you done?" I said, "I have just stuck the Pittsburgh coach half the distance of the goal for unsportsmanlike conduct. Put that ball on the nine yard line and give Dallas a first down!" He said, "Yes, and I have to walk it off!" I said, "That's the penalty of leadership — walk."

Then, the greatest thing that ever happened to me in my 15 year career of professional football happened. On the next play, Staubauch went back to pass, hit Drew Pearson in the end zone right on the numbers and he dropped it. If he hadn't dropped that ball I wouldn't be writing this today. I'd be pushing up marble in some cemetery!

Why do I tell you that story? I tell you that story because four weeks later the National Football League sent me back to Pittsburgh to work that championship game between Pittsburgh and Houston. Nobody decides who's going to work where in this league, except the league office in New York. The officials are rated every week. They're rated by a man in the press box. That's what I do now. They're rated off the films in the New York office as well as by both coaches. Four ratings a week are made and at the end of the year they add up those ratings. If you're rated number one in your position, you work the Super Bowl and wear one of these rings that I proudly wear. If you're rated second or third you work the championship game and so on down the line. You see, we in the National Football League, like you in business and in life, pay off on excellence!

We pay off on excellence. So, back I went to Pittsburgh to work that championship game. I had worked the Super Bowl the year before when Dallas beat Denver and I guess I was rated second or third my last year. So, I went back to Pittsburgh to work that championship game and I haven't been there since I stuck Mr. Noll with the only unsportsmanlike conduct call he's ever had.

I got out to the ball park about eleven o'clock in the morning, two hours before the game. I was dressed in a business suit. I walked into his office and he got up from behind his desk, walked around, stuck his hand out, smiled and said, "Art, congratulations." I said, "Thanks, coach. The same to you." He asked, "What do you want?" I said, "I gotta get my legs taped." He said, "Come on, I'll take you over to the training room."

We walked over and talked about our families, the weather, the game and never once did that great coach mention that call. He was able to take it, wrap it up in a box, put it on a shelf, learn from it, and forget about it. We walked into the training room. Some big lineman was laying there getting taped, two or three other big guys were waiting and Noll said to the trainer, "Get this guy off of here. Art's got some pre-game duties to do." I got up and they started to tape my legs. Coach Noll started to leave, I said, "Coach, wait a minute. You're the head coach of a championship team in a championship game and you take the time, the attention to detail to see that I get my legs taped. I just want you to know that I appreciate it." He said, "Art, I want to tell you something. When you're the head man, you got to be a detail man, an organizer, a communicator and a delegator. By the way, Mean Joe Greene wants to talk with you about that call in the Dallas game!"

He walked out and standing right beside me was Big Jack Lambert, the big red bearded linebacker for the Pittsburgh Steelers. He's retired now. I don't know Lambert off the field, he may be a great guy. But, I'm going to tell you one thing, when Lambert put on pads he had no friends. I've had a lot of fouls against Lambert. So he took one look at me and said, "It's you again!" I said, "That's right, Lambert." He said, "Every time we get a big football game we get you and your yellow flag against the Pittsburgh Steelers." I said, "Lambert, just knock it off, I'll see you out on the field in two hours. Get out of here!" You got to take command—foolish as it was. He turned around, walked about two steps, turned around again, and with a big grin on his face said, "I'll say one thing, Art, you're the second best football official in the national football league." I felt good. I said, "Who's first?" He said, "The other 98 are tied!"

What I'm saying to you is if you're in second place don't get too smug. Everybody else might be tied for first and that makes you last. There's only one place to finish in this world and that's on top! That's what the challenge of professionalism is all about—to be on the top—all of the time.

Vince Lombardi, who coached the Green Bay Packers, said, "It takes talent to become a champion, but it takes character to stay there." I want to paraphrase a quote from the immortal Vince Lombardi. He said, "Being a pro is not a sometime thing. It's an all the time thing. You're not a pro once in a while, you don't do things right once in a while, you do them right all the time. Being a pro, a winner; is a habit. Every time a football player goes out on the field to ply his trade he's got to play from the ground up; he's got to play from the soles of his feet right up to his head. Every inch of him has to play." It's the same in business and in life. If you're a pro, you're a pro 24 hours a day.

So what's this challenge all about? Number one, respond to change. People say to me, "I can't change." I tell them baloney. The Lord gave us the power of choice. When we get up in the morning, we can be happy or sad, productive or unproductive; it's up to us. I was talking the other day to a group of young bankers. I asked one of the young men, "How long have you worked for the bank?" He said, "Ever since the day they threatened to fire me." He didn't know how fast he could change!

Football is a game of change. If the quarterback calls a "49 sweep" in the huddle (that's the fullback wide right), comes up to the line of scrimmage and sees the defense set against the play, does he buck his head against a stone wall? Of course not. He uses his individual God-given power of choice and calls an audible. He reaches down, tickles the center (that's what they do, that's why they all want to be centers, it feels so good) and says, "48 blue, tax reform." I don't know what that means, I don't think congress does either. He says, "48 blue, tax reform." When 10 other offensive guys hear those words, "tax reform," they say, "Hey, that's not a 49 sweep anymore that's a square out pass." The split end out there says, "I don't block the linebacker anymore, I go down four steps, turn to the left, the quarterback throws me the ball, I catch it and go for a first down or a touchdown." Why? Because he had the ability to change.

We had a game in San Diego between San Diego and the former Oakland Raiders about eight years ago. John Madden was the coach of the Oakland Raiders. I was the line judge. I was on the line of scrimmage opposite the head linesman. The head linesman and the line judge keep track of the line of scrimmage. That's our territory. Tony Veteri was the head linesman, positioned in front of the Oakland bench, while I was opposite him in front of the San Diego bench.

Now the question is, how many men do you have to have on a line of scrimmage in football? Answer? Seven. If you have six it's a foul. Why is that important? If you catch a team like Dallas, they'll take the slot man over on the right, bring him up from the line of scrimmage and drop the wide receiver off. Or, they'll take the tight end over on the left, drop him back and bring the flanker up. Sometimes somebody forgets a signal and you end up with six guys on a line then you throw the flag. The question further arises, "can you legally have eight men on the line?" Answer, "yes," "Nine?" "Sure." "Ten?" "Absolutely." You only have to have one man in the backfield. But,what do you see play after play, game after game? You see seven men on the line of scrimmage.

Human beings are creatures of habit. We like to do it the same today as we did it yesterday so we can do it the same tomorrow. Because the rut gets comfortable. But, the only difference between a rut and a grave is it's length, depth and how long you're in it!!

Tony and I had worked more than 200 football games in the NFL, but we had never seen an eight man line. In the second quarter the game was scoreless. It was Oakland's ball, third and eight on their own 40. Out of the huddle they come. Stabler brings them up to the line and I count eight guys on the line. Not trusting myself when I get over five, I counted them again. I still got eight. They set for a second, which the offense must do on every play. After they had set for a second, 88 out there on the end of the line turned and went in motion, diagonally into his own backfield.

My wheels were turning. I know that one man for the offense may be in motion, parallel to or away from his line of scrimmage. But can he come from the line of scrimmage? I don't think so. That's not good enough! Oakland snapped the ball, I threw the flag—not too high!! Ben Tompkins, our back judge, yelled out, "Great call Art." My confidence level went up. Stabler completed a pass for 25 yards and a first down. I came running in, "No, bring it back, illegal motion." Veteri came running over from the other side, "What is it?" I said, "Illegal motion." He said, "Art, he's going backwards." I said, "Tony, he came from the end of the line." He said, "So." And he shrugged.

A shrug is not a signal in football. It's also not a good sales tool. He said, "So." I said, "So, it's illegal. Go tell him!" I don't want to talk to Madden. I'm smarter than that! I'm over on the San Diego side and they think it's a great call! They don't know why, they just think it's great! Well, we bring the ball back. Oakland has to punt. Five minutes later Oakland has the ball again.

Now they got third and 13, back on their own 30. Out of the huddle they came—up the line of scrimmage—and I counted eight men on the line with 88 out on the end again. They set for a second. Now 88 knows he fouled last time because he heard his number over the PA system. But he doesn't know why. So, this time he's taking no chances. He turns around, goes in motion straight backwards, he's going out of the ball park! They snapped the ball, I threw the flag a mile in the air. Stabler completed a 50 yard bomb to Cliff Branch—a leaping catch down on the other 25 yard line! I came running in, "No, bring it back—illegal motion." Veteri comes running over from the other side and says, "Art, what in the world are you doing?" I said, "Tony, it's illegal for that guy to go in motion from the end of that line." He said, "Well, you go tell him!!"

Now Madden's over there going "Boidflklk, jsuiofg;l." He's selling Lite Beer. I went over and he said, "Art, what in the world are you doing to us?" I said, "John, it's illegal for that player to go in motion from the end of that line." And *this* is what he said, "Art, this is our secret play! It's the only thing we've practiced all week!" I said, "You run that thing 10 times today, I'm gonna throw 10 flags." We went into the half. What was the first thing I did before I did anything else? I grabbed the rule book. You can't carry that thing on the field, it's bulky and it looks funny to say, "Just a second and I'll look that up."

Here's what it says football fans. "After all 11 players for the offense come to a full one second stop, one offensive player may be in motion, parallel to, or away from his line of scrimmage and he must be a backfield player." A backfield player is defined as one who has set for at least one second at least one yard off the ball." Great call! Naturally! But somewhere, sometime, somebody had said to me, "In order to legally be in motion you have to set for one second in that backfield," and that tiny piece of information had stuck with me and prepared me for change.

What will you take from this chapter to help you respond to change, to anticipate change in this time of the most rapidly changing society the world has ever known? Microtechnology, computers, robotics, all kinds of changes are happening all around us. Can you respond to it—and even more important—can you be a *cause* of change!

As you talk about excellence and talk about professionalism, do you know where discipline fits into a successful operation? I'm the symbol of discipline on the football field. Somebody has to make the rules, somebody else has to enforce them. There's also the discipline of self-discipline. The toughest discipline in the world. Doing what I'm supposed to do, when I'm supposed to do it, where I'm supposed to do it as the line judge in the National Football League.

Let me tell you a true story. I worked the only professional football game played at the University of Michigan Stadium in Ann Arbor. It was a pre-season game between the Detroit Lions and the Baltimore Colts. It was 93 degrees with 80 percent relative humidity. The temperature of the artificial turf was 148 degrees. Standing on the sideline before the game was the referee. He was about to referee his first game in the National Football League. He had been a line judge and been moved to referee. He turned to me and said, "Art, are you scared?" I said, "No, I'm up, I'm not scared." He said, "I've got a little knot in my stomach." I said, "Let me ask you a question. There are 93,000 people here, over 90 ball players, all the coaching staffs and the other five officials in this game. Can you name one that is more competent to referee this game than you?" He said, "No." I said, "You're it baby—and I've got one more question to ask you. Do you think that you can referee one play right in the National Football League?" He said, "Of course." I said, "I've got a secret to tell you. That's the only way they'll ever play this game, one play at a time."

You see it's one customer at a time, one chance to reflect

the advertising of a company. One chance at a time and that's where it's at. If you work one play right and then the next one and then the next one, pretty soon it's a game. Then it's a season. Then it's the Super Bowl. Don't you see? And, you do that in a teamwork environment—football is very much a team sport, there's a sense of loyalty. I'd like to talk about the discipline of loyalty.

The most severe criticism a football official ever receives is when seven football officials, alone on a Saturday night, look at 10 rolls of slow motion film of the game they worked the previous week, along with a critique sheet from New York. That's when you hear the most severe criticism. I remember a game in Chicago between the Bears and Green Bay Packers. I called a clip against the Bears that took the winning touchdown away from them. Clipping is blocking from the rear; blocking from the side is not a clip and this was one of those "iffy" ones. The next week, we're in New Orleans on a Saturday night at the Mariott Hotel. There were six officials at that time watching five rolls of slow motion film with a play by play critique sheet of the game and they had a big red question mark by that play with a comment, "check this, we don't think it's a clip!" We ran it four times, four of the guys on the crew were "iffy" on the thing, but the head linesman with whom I differed occasionally, jumped up and said, "Art, that wasn't a clip." I said, "Tony, it was a clip." I was on a short fuse and we ended up toe to toe and had to be pulled apart!

I've seen that many times. But, I'm going to tell you something. I've never seen one football official in the National Football League show up another one on the field. If that Back Judge calls some little bump pass interference, and the guy couldn't have caught the ball with a butterfly net, you don't see the field judge come running over and saying, "My God, Burt, how could you have called that?" He'll come over nod, smile, and say, "Burt—dummy, pick up your flag. He couldn't have caught it with a net!" That's loyalty—working together.

What I'm saying is that a part of excellence, a part of

professionalism, is loyalty to your organization. Loyalty to the people who work around you, for you, under you or over you. Loyalty to your products, to your people and to your friends.

Number three. Are you a problem solver? We've got a lot of problem finders today. We've got a Ralph Nader syndrome: find something wrong with everything. Sure you got problems. Interest rates yo-yoing all over the place, economy soft, economy hard, gold prices down, gold prices up, too much competition, all of that. You could have it worse. Football is a problem solving game. I went to Knox College in Galesburg, Illinois. Most of you never heard of it. I enrolled during 1939.

We were famous athletically for one thing — 28 consecutive football losses. We led the world in football losses. When I was a freshman we broke that record and I'm proud of it. I'm going to tell you how it was. We were getting beat as usual in the fourth quarter. We were down, 21 — 20 with four minutes to go in the ball game when somebody in the stands threw a firecracker. The other team ran off the field! Eight plays later we scored — on a field goal that was partially blocked.

The problem in football is, how are you going to get the ball from one end of the field to the other and in your possession? And if you're on defense, how are you going to stop the other team? How are you going to relate features to benefits to sell better than the other salesperson? How are you going to make a product better? How are you going to deliver it better? How are you going to help solve the problems of your customers? How are you going to not only respond to them, but anticipate them?

That's why God gave us this ability to think creatively. To solve our own problems and others. That's how we earn our keep for the space that we take up on earth.

There are problems everywhere. They even have problems in church. I used to go to a little Lutheran Church in Minnesota. It had one of those high choir lofts. It also had one of those women who sing soprano — who could hit high

C. They always reach for it like it's an orange on a tree! They go right up after it! One Sunday, she went after that high C and head first she went right out of the choir loft. On the way down, her foot caught in the chandelier and there she was, swinging in front of the congregation with her dress hanging down over her head. The minister was equal to the occasion. He leaped to his feet and said, "The first man that looks at her will be struck blind." Ollie and Sven, two old Swedes, were sitting right down on the front row. Ollie poked Sven and said, "You know Sven, I think I'm gonna risk one eye."

Risk in business, risk in our free way of life. But I'll tell you one fundamental truth. You can't have reward in one hand without being willing to take risks in the other. And sometimes after you leave the collective society of a team, you reach the point as a pro where you have to make an individual decision.

Let me tell you a story. I worked the game in Chicago when Gale Sayers ran for six touchdowns against the San Francisco 49er's in 1965. It was the greatest performance I've ever seen by a running back. Everybody will remember that—it's in the Hall of Fame. My only claim to fame, my only appearance in the Hall of Fame was on film following Sayers down the field at quite a distance.

But something else happened in that game that only four of us will remember. In the late third quarter San Francisco had the ball and ran a running play around the strong side around the tight end. He made about eight yards. I was the back judge. I blew the whistle, put my foot down and as I lifted my head and blew the whistle the tight end from San Francisco blocked Mike Reilly, number 65, the outside linebacker for the Chicago Bears—265 pounds, 26 years old, fully armored with helmet and shoulder pads. He knocked Reilly off balance and as I looked up I saw this football player coming at me. I'm five feet nine—170 pounds—knit shirt—lovable. I had a problem and I couldn't call the office!

I had to make a decision and I made it. I reached up instinctively and grabbed Reilly by the face mask, I know why that's a foul because that face mask is a great lever. As I went over backwards, I yanked his head down into the mud beside me and he never touched me. He leaped to his feet ran to the 49er that blocked him and said, "You so-and-so, you didn't have to grab me by the face mask." I jumped in between them and said, "Come on, Mike, cut it out. He didn't mean it." Bill Schleibaum was the line judge, he came running up and said, "Art, if I knew which way to walk I'd throw the flag on you." Problem solving; thinking fast.

Number four. Do you know where teamwork fits into a professional operation? Teamwork means respect for the dignity and differences in people. In a time when there are those in our society who would like to put us all into one big bucket, shake us up and have us come out as average Americans—divide the wealth, divide the brains, divide everything; I am proud to be part of a sport that does not pay off on averages. We don't play average teams in the Super Bowl. We play the best and we don't care who knows it.

But a part of that team work, a part of responsibility in that team work, is to look for your weakest link. I can't tell you how many times I've looked at films where 10 guys on offense did it right but one guy blew a signal on what should have been a touchdown and went for a three yard loss. A part of the responsibility of a pro is to look not only for your own weaknesses but for those around you in order to strengthen them or get rid of them.

Next question. Do you understand successful failure? Football is a game of failure. A guy learns to get knocked down and then get right back up. If he keeps getting up maybe he blocks the punt and wins the ball game. It takes a mature attitude toward failure. I have a deal with the preachers, priests and rabbis, I don't monkey with the first 10 commandments. I leave that to the pros. But I handle the 11th.

The 11th commandment is, "Thou shalt not take thyself too seriously." Can you laugh at yourself? It's the second greatest God- given gift. The first one is the ability to think creatively—to be able to respond to change or cause change, to solve problems. Then secondly—we are the only animal with the ability to laugh. I guess He figured that when reason failed if we couldn't laugh, we'd all end up in a looney bin. And in this game of the most violent competition you'll ever see, right under that veneer of competition lies a sense of humor.

I spoke at the Cleveland Browns Touchdown banquet a few years ago and Art Model, the owner of the Cleveland Browns, a great sportsman and owner, was sitting next to me and told me this story. "Brian Sipe was our quarterback a couple years ago and he was having a terrible year. He was leading the league in interceptions — we were two and 12. We were playing Dallas and we were down 40 to 10 with two games left to go in the season — the season is gone. Sipe has thrown five interceptions in the game then he threw his sixth. As he's coming off the field, with his helmet in his hand and his head down, Sam Rutigliano (the Brown's Coach) — reached out and grabbed him by the arm and said, "Brian, why are you throwing the ball to them?" And Sipes said, "Because they're the only ones open!" The ability to laugh at yourself.

You see, you don't close every sale. Creative sales people lose sales. But they know the two "L's" of failure; to learn and laugh at failure. When we're creative — when we try to meet tomorrow in a creative way, sometimes it doesn't work. And sometimes even when we respond to something today it doesn't work. I sent flowers to a friend of mine who opened a new branch of his business to be nice. I went out to call on him and look for my flowers. There's a big wreath with a sash on it that said 'Rest In Peace.' I went out of there and called the florist. I said, "What in the devil are you doing? I send the guy flowers to wish him well in business and you send him a wreath that says Rest In Peace!" He says, "I'm not worried about you Art. Somewhere in this town there's a man being buried and he's got a big bouquet of roses with a sash on it that says 'Good Luck in Your New Location.'"

Part of the challenge of excellence is to wear a smile on your face. One of the greatest sales tools ever given to man or woman is hung between the point of the nose and the tip of the chin. It's called a big friendly smile that says, "I like you,

I want to help you. I am quality. I represent quality in my service, quality in my product and, most of all, I care about you." Because people don't care how much you know until they know how much you care.

Last question. Do you believe in the principle of added values? When iron ore comes out of the Mesabi range in Minnesota it's a red dust. It'll get your shoes dirty, it's worthless. We add value to it, spend money on it and ship it across the great lakes to Pittsburgh. We put it through a blast furnace, add more value, spend more money. It comes out as various kinds of steel. We ship it back to Detroit and pickle it, tool it, paint it, put rubber on it, wrap glass around it and advertise it. That worthless red dust shows up in your driveway and mine as a six, eight, ten thousand dollar automobile. Value has been added all along the way.

But—there's a similar principle of added values in human beings. The professional not only knows about added values in products, the professional knows about adding values to human beings. He gives those people around him the opportunity to live up to their potential.

So, I want to close with a poem. An old one that's a favorite of mine.

"Twas battered and scarred and the auctioneer thought it barely worth his while—to spend much time with the old violin. But he held it up with a smile. "What am I bidden, good folks?" he cried, "who'll start the bidding for me? A dollar? A dollar—who'll make it two? Two dollars, who'll make it three? Three dollars once—three dollars twice, going for three." But no! From the back of the room a gray haired man came forward and picked up the bow. He wiped the dust from the old violin—tightened its old loose strings, and played a melody as pure and sweet as a caroling Angel sings.

The music ceased and the auctioneer, in a voice that was quiet and low, said, "What am I bid for the old violin?" He held it up with the bow. "A thousand dollars! Who'll make it two? Two thousand — who'll make it three? Three thousand once — three thousand twice and going and gone," said he.

The people cheered, but some of them cried, "We do not quite understand. What changed it's value?" Swift came the reply, "The touch of a masters hand!"

And many a man with life out-of-tune — battered and scarred with sin, is auctioned cheap by the thoughtless crowd, much like the old violin. A mess of pottage — glass of wine — a game, and he travels on. He's going once — going twice — he's going and almost gone.

Then the master comes and the foolish crowd never can quite understand — the worth of a soul and the change that's wrought by the touch of the master's hand.

You are good — I know you are — but the question is not "how good are you?" The question is, "how good can you be?" Because you see, no matter how good you are, you are never, never so good that you can't be better. That's the challenge of a professional, that's what excellence is all about. Go for it, good luck and God bless you.

12

PACKING PARACHUTES

Charles Plumb
1200 N. San Marcos Rd.
Santa Barbara, CA 93111
805/683-1969

My first prison cell in Vietnam was eight feet long and eight feet wide. I could pace three steps one way and three steps the other. Inside the cell there were no books to read, no window to look out; no TV, telephone or radio. I didn't have a real pencil or a piece of paper for 2,103 days. I didn't have a roommate for several months.

What I had was three steps one way and three steps the other. I was going stir crazy in that cell. I finally decided, "Charlie, you must come up with something to do or you're going to go nuts in here". So I made a little game to play. I constructed a little deck of playing cards about the size of postage stamps. I tore these cards from 52 strips of toilet paper. And I can tell you this with authority; it's tough to shuffle toilet paper!

Recently, my wife Cathy and I were sitting in a restaurant. A man about two tables away kept looking at me. I didn't recognize him. A few minutes into our meal he stood up and walked over to our table, looked down at me, pointed his finger in my face and said, "You're Plumb." I looked up and I said, "Yes, sir, I'm Plumb." He said, "You flew jet fighters in Vietnam. You were on the aircraft carrier *Kitty Hawk*. You were shot down. You parachuted into enemy hands and spent six years as a prisoner of war."

I said, "How in the world did you know that?" He replied, "I packed your parachute."

I staggered to my feet and held out a very grateful hand of thanks. I was speechless. This guy came up with just the proper words. He grabbed my hand, pumped my arm and said, "I guess it worked." "Yes, sir, indeed it did," I said, "and I must tell you I've said a lot of prayers of thanks for your nimble fingers, but I never thought I'd have the opportunity to express my gratitude in person."

He said, "Were all the panels there?"

"Well, sir, I must shoot straight with you," I said, "of the 18 panels, that were supposed to be in that parachute, I had 15 good ones. Three were torn, but it wasn't your fault, it was mine. I jumped out of that jet fighter at a high rate of speed, close to the ground. That's what tore the panels in the parachute, it wasn't the way you packed it. "

I didn't get much sleep that night. I kept thinking about that man. I kept wondering what he might have looked like in a navy uniform — a dixie cup hat, a bib in the back and bell bottom trousers. I wondered how many times I might have passed him on board the *Kitty Hawk*. I wondered how many times I might have seen him and not even said good morning, how are you or anything because, you see, I was a fighter pilot and he was just a sailor. How many hours did he spend on that long wooden table in the bowels of that ship weaving the shrouds and folding the silks of those chutes, doing a standard (or even mediocre) job? I could have cared less...until one day *my* parachute came along and he packed mine for me.

So the philosophical question is "Who's packing your parachute?" Everybody needs someone to pack their parachute. We all need that kind of support in time of need. We all need those who step out in front and say, "Yes, I'll help."

My parachute was well packed when I was shot down over enemy territory. My physical parachute, my mental parachute, my emotional parachute and my spiritual parachute were pretty well in place.

All that parachute packing began in a very small town in Kansas. I loved that town. My parachute was packed by my Dad, my Mom, my big sister, my two little brothers and a coach named Smith.

Clancy Smith was a 65 year old World War I veteran. He was a tough hombre who still had some shrapnel in one leg. He walked with a limp. We were the last team he ever coached and unfortunately, we didn't have a very good season. Our record was one and seven. We wanted to win that last game for him, but we lost. I'll never forget walking back to the locker room and Coach Smith came up and put his arm over my sweaty shoulder. I looked up at him and said, "I'm sorry coach, I guess we're just a bunch of losers." He squeezed my shoulder, sunk his fingers into my flesh and said, "Son, whether you think you're a loser or whether you think you're a winner...you're right."

The next day at school I said, "Coach, I don't understand what you meant. Would you explain it to me?"

He said, "Son, I don't want you to come back here in four or five years and tell me the reason you failed in high school and college was because you didn't learn anything in this little county school. I don't want you coming back here in six or eight years and telling me that the reason you couldn't get a job was because you weren't educated. I don't want you telling me in 12 or 14 years the reason you failed was because you married the wrong girl." He said, "What makes the difference between your success or failure is *you*. It's a choice. You can choose success, you can choose failure, or you can *choose to give away the choice.*

I graduated from that little grade school and I went away to Annapolis, the Naval Academy, where I was held prisoner! They let me go after four years, but I got my parachute packed there too. Admiral Charles Kirkpatrick was the Commandant of Midshipmen. He would stand up in front of the big pep rallies and clench his fists so tight you could see the veins run in his brow, and he'd say, "You guys can do anything you set your mind to do." That became our motto. For four years we didn't know how to lose. And we didn't very often. We were the number two and number one team in the nation. Best of all, Navy beat Army four times straight!

Uncle Charlie was right. We *could* do anything we set our minds to do!

I graduated from Annapolis, married my high school sweetheart and was sent to Flight Training. Two and a half years later I was qualified to pilot the F-4B Phantom jet, the hottest fighter plane in the world, and set sail on the aircraft carrier *Kitty Hawk* for Vietnam.

After 75 combat missions, on the 19th of May, my jet fighter was hit by a surface to air missile. The radar interceptor officer in my back seat and I started to tumble through the sky. We found ourselves upside down going down at 500 miles per hour — a screaming fireball headed for the ground. My co-pilot was getting a little concerned! He said, "You want to get out, Charlie?" "Wait a minute," I said. "We have this extra special problem." The way you normally get out of a jet fighter is with an ejection seat. It's like a rocket under your chair. Set off the rocket and it shoots the chair out the top of the airplane. We were upside down. To eject from that altitude upside down would have planted us about six and a half feet below the level of the rice paddy.

I had to turn the airplane upright. I grabbed the stick but it was frozen. I'd lost all my hydraulics. The only control I had left was a manual rudder. I hit that rudder as hard as I could. The airplane shuddered, rolled back upright and we ejected. We came floating down in our parachutes over enemy territory.

Ever been in one of those parachutes? I don't mean the silk and nylon kind, I'm talking about those parachutes of life. I'm talking about those times when your gut is twisted and wrenched with a decision you have to make and none of the decisions seem quite right. I'm talking about those fender benders, the hang nails, the little things that get to us.

The parachute opened. I looked at my co-pilot, he was in good shape, and then I bowed my head and said a prayer. I asked for strength from above.

We drifted down to the ground and were captured immediately and hauled into the prison camp. I was tortured for military information and political propaganda. After two days of that they put me in the cell, the one I described to you at the beginning. It was in fact eight feet long and eight feet wide. Now, I was moved around to several cells during my captivity — some were larger, some were smaller, but the first cell and the average cell was 8x8. I could, in fact, take three steps one way and three steps the other. I was afraid. I feared not only for my life but for the lives of my buddies. I feared for those who were at home waiting for me; my wife, my family and friends.

I was pacing along back and forth across that cell. I was well into my 200th mile when I heard, in the far corner, the chirping noise of a cricket. I paid no attention at first. Yet the longer I listened to the cricket the more rhythmic it became.

"Now, that's a pretty educated little critter." I thought to myself, "Maybe I can teach that dude to sing." So I walked over to the corner and found it wasn't a cricket at all but a piece of wire. It was about four inches long and was coming out of a hole at the base of the cell wall and scratching on my concrete floor making a chirping noise like a cricket. I watched the wire bobbing in and out of the wall for quite a while.

I figured the wire had to be connected to an American on the other end, maybe on the other side of the storeroom next to my cell. I needed to communicate with another American. By that time in my experience I was losing track of what was a real memory and what was just a hallucination. I needed to tug on the wire.

But, the overriding emotion was fear. I was afraid to tug on the wire. I was sure that on the other end there was going to be another macho fighter pilot who was stronger than I and who wouldn't understand the condition I was in (and he probably didn't cry when they tortured him). I was 24 years old, a jet fighter pilot, the guy who was supposed to have "the right stuff."

I was a graduate from the Naval Academy, an Officer in the greatest Navy in the world. But, I had 27 boils on my front side and a bunch more on my back. I was bleeding from four open wounds from the torture. I was in the prime of my youth, but I was down to 115 pounds, rotting away in a communist prison camp. My sole possession in life, was a rag I had knotted around my waist to hide my nudity. I didn't want anyone else, least of all one of my peers, to see me the way I saw myself.

Ever had that kind of fear? I guess we all do some times. We're all afraid once in a while to tug on a wire. We're all afraid once in a while to offer to pack that parachute.

Finally, I got the guts up to do it. I knelt down in the prison cell and reached for the wire. I tugged on it three times and it tugged back three times. I tugged again and it tugged again. I tugged four times and it disappeared. Well, I stepped back in the cell wondering what would happen next. The little wire came back about an hour later. Wrapped around the end of the wire was a little note. It was made of toilet paper. Just blobs of ashes on this wadded up piece of toilet paper. It said, "Memorize this code, then eat this note." I did. I memorized the code, ate the note. I knelt down again at the hole in the wall and started tugging on the little wire. On the other end of the wire was Lieutenant Commander Bob Schumacher fighter pilot and astronaut candidate and best of all, a "Parachute Packer." He'd been there two years when I arrived. His first words were, "How you doing, buddy?"

That was my cue. I'd been looking for someone to tell my troubles to so I said, "I'm doing terrible, buddy." I said, "My president sent me over here and I got shot down in his beautiful little war. Then some idiot mechanic didn't put a transistor in the airplane. Get Congress over here. They're the ones who appropriated all the money. Let them sit in this prison camp. I am the victim of circumstances beyond my control. I'm going to rot away and die in here because of someone else's mistake. Help me!"

He said, "You want to know your biggest problem?"

I thought, "You mean I got problems bigger than the ones I can see?"

"It sure sounds like it," he said. "It sounds like you're suffering from a fairly common disease that can kill you if you don't catch it in time."

I said, "What's the name of this disease, maybe I know something about it."

He said, "Around here we call it 'prison thinking.'"

I said, "Prison thinking?"

He said, "Roger. You *think* you're a prisoner."

I thought, what kind of nut did they put me next to? This guy's in space somewhere. He doesn't know how badly I hurt. But, I had to keep communicating, I had to keep tugging on the wire. I said, "Tell me about 'prison thinking.'"

He said, "Well, when a guy gets shot down, the very normal red-blooded American thing for him to do is start feeling sorry for himself and blaming everybody else." He said, "You go into the 'woe is me' mode of life. 'Woe is me, poor mama Plumb's little boy Charlie is a long way from home in a communist prison camp.' You get a bushel of pity and then just wallow in it. Then you start blaming everybody you can think of. Blame your president for sending you over here, blame Congress for appropriating the money, blame your mechanic for putting your airplane together, blame your mother for giving you birth. The problem with this, of course, is that when you start blaming other people for your misfortune you suddenly give them control over your life." And it hit me, that's what the coach was saying years before. I do have the choice. I control my own destiny.

I must admit, it took me a long time to validate that principle. I'm still working on it today. I get out here on the highway, I'm driving down the road minding my own business doing 55 right on the double nickel. Some idiot comes around me and cuts me off. I hit my horn, I hit my brake, I wave my fist, I yell some obscenity and all day long I'm stirring up all those cholesterols, see, getting ready for a good old heart attack. While the guy that cut me off is just driving right on down the road. Doesn't even know my name and yet he's got control of my life.

I said, "Okay, Schumacher. You've got my attention. Now tell me, what's the antidote for this disease?"

He said, "Well, the first thing you need to break down the walls of prison thinking is faith. Not just spiritual faith, you also have to have faith in your country and faith in your roots. The second thing you need while you're here is commitment. You've got to be committed to a set of standards you can't be afraid to stand up and tell the world what you think is right. The third thing you need is PRIDE."

I said, "Pride." I looked at my poor wretched body again.

"That's right, pride. You've got to be proud of yourself. You've got to believe you're a good enough person you can overcome all the problems and, one of these days, march out of here a proud American, with your head held high."

I said, "Okay, I think I've got those things — faith, commitment, pride."

I found during the next six years that those three factors were more important than the rice we ate or the water we drank. Schumacher sure packed my parachute that day. He gave me the panels which allowed me to overcome the adversity of prison life, but he certainly wasn't the only one to do it. If we hadn't been involved in a fellowship of prisoners of war I don't think I'd be alive today.

One of the greatest parachute packers of all in that camp was an enlisted man. Most of us, as you know, were officers and pilots, we had very few enlisted men in the prison camps in Vietnam, and yet, one guy was there. He was a Navy sailor. How did a Navy sailor get into a prison camp in an air war in Asia? He fell off his ship and got washed ashore! Try to explain that to your commanding officer.

"Seaman Douglas Hegdahl from Clark, South Dakota." He had enlisted in the Navy when he was 17 and they sent him off to a place that he couldn't even pronounce. Late one night he fell off the back of his ship. He floated around for six hours, finally washed ashore, was captured and put into a prison camp 10,000 miles away from home in a communist country where he had to live with 200 macho fighter pilots — which may have been the worst part of all.

Young Hegdahl could take a joke. He was a Radar O'Reilly kind of a kid. What a parachute packer! We'd have these contests. We'd tug on the wire and tap on the wall in our secret code. We'd say, "Who's the oldest in the prison camp," or "Who's been here the longest," or "Who's got the most children back home?" One time we had what we called the "High Fast — Low Slow" contest to determine what pilot had ejected from his airplane highest and fastest, who had gone out lowest and slowest. Well, High Fast was won by some Air Force jock who punched out of his F-105 at 52,000 feet at 1,000 miles an hour. The Low Slow contest was won by Seaman Hegdahl — 12 feet at 15 knots.

About three years into my stay, the North Vietnamese were getting a lot of flack from the World press about their treatment of prisoners and their torture techniques. So they decided to release some guys early as proof of their good will. Most of us were given an opportunity to go home early. But we had a code: the Code of Conduct. It's not a military regulation, it's only a code. You can't be court marshalled for violating it. And yet, we knew the strength of our unity, so we elected not to accept early release. Our senior man selected Seaman Hegdahl to go home. Why? Hegdahl was the youngest person there, and an enlisted man; but more importantly, Hegdahl had developed a photographic memory in that prison camp. He'd gone through the list of 200 prisoners and memorized their first, middle and last names. He memorized our next of kin and then each hometown of each of the relatives. Finally, he memorized the telephone numbers of each of the relatives of each of the 200 prisoners of war.

Well, Seaman Hegdahl came home. Here's a nineteen year old lad, a sailor with two years back pay in his pocket, hadn't seen a girl in two years and he's free on the streets of San Diego. Remember, he's a parachute packer. He started to travel. He went from the West Coast to the East Coast. He spent his own time and a lot of his own money. He went North to South. He went through each of the hometowns he'd memorized. He spoke to each of the relatives he'd memorized and told them that their prisoner was alive. Doug Hegdahl wasn't looking for a great kudo or accolade. No achievement medals were given for what he was doing.

We wondered for six years how we'd find out we were going home. Finally they told us. A peace treaty was signed and a POW exchange was underway. We launched out of there on an Air Force C-141. What a sight that was — I had a big lump in my throat — the American flag on the side of the airplane. Wow! Our first stop was Clarke Air Force base in the Philippines. I made a telephone call I'd been wanting to make for six years — to my wife in Kansas. And she had gone. I called my Dad. "Dad, what's happened to my wife?"

He said, "Come on home son, and we'll talk about that face to face."

I said, "Dad, it's going to take me three days to get back. Tell me now, will you? What's happened?" My father couldn't do it so he passed the telephone to my mother. I'll never forget her words.

She said, "Son, I'd give ten years of my life if I didn't have to tell you this. Your wife filed for divorce...just three months ago. She's engaged to another man."

I returned to Kansas City and found lots of well-meaning people giving me advice. The legal advisors were saying, "Sue her and her boyfriend. We've got the papers all written out (which they did). Just sign right here. We're going to put him in jail. We're going to take them for all they're worth. That'll fix them." Psychiatrists and psychologists had some pretty good ideas too. They were saying, "Charlie, you've got to get angry about this. You've got to get all this stuff out of your system. If anybody has the right to be bitter, you do."

Imagine that. Somebody telling me I have the right to be bitter. I'm saying to myself, "Now wait a minute. I fully admit I am a Rip Van Winkle awakened after six years. I really don't know exactly what's going on here, but I have been through six years of the "University of Hanoi." And I got a degree in hard knocks. But, if there's one single thing I validated in that communist prison camp it's this: Coach Smith was right. It *is* my choice. I can choose to be bitter, and maybe that's the easiest choice. I can choose to sue everybody I can think of. I can choose to be really angry. I can choose to crawl over in the corner and die and I *know* I can do that. I have that capability, I've seen men do it. Or, I have another choice. Pick up the pieces of this great jigsaw puzzle, press on with my life with the confidence and the commitment that it's going to take and live every day to the fullest, regardless of the price." That's what I've done, and that's what the other men have done too. You know who we are, you read about us in the papers. The ex-POW's from Vietnam are alive and well.

We had a POW reunion recently in Washington. We're setting records. So far we've produced two U.S. Senators. We have state legislators all over the country. We have bishops, judges, teachers, doctors, lawyers, professional pilots and public speakers. The medical community tells us we're healthier today, mentally and physically, than the men who didn't get shot down. Schumacher, the guy on the end of the wire, is a three star Admiral today. Doug Hegdahl, the kid who memorized the names, has a masters degree and is teaching. My ex-wife went ahead and married the fellow she was engaged to. I bounced around the Country as a bachelor for a lot of years. I married a gal from Memphis, Tennessee. We have a handsome son and a beautiful daughter.

But what's the connection? You'll never be a prisoner of war, you'll never have to pace three steps one direction and then turn around and pace three steps the other. You'll never have to learn all of those codes. But, don't you see the similarity? Each of us has a choice. We have the choice to stand up and be counted for what we think is right. We have the choice to give of ourselves and pack those parachutes. We have a choice to be part of the team. When you get older and look back on your life, you don't count dollars, you count the parachutes you packed.

Six years is a long time to pace three steps one direction and three steps the other. I wouldn't wish it on anyone. And yet, I would tell you it's the most valuable six years of my life. Amazing what a little adversity can teach a person. It gives a man a pause to think, "How will I survive? What are the techniques of survival, what are the properties of a winner?" There's no bed of roses. You'll have some mountains to climb and some parachutes to pack and you'll have to tug on some wires along the way. You'll have to apply the faith, the commitment and the personal pride. But if you can put those basic principles together as part of your daily discipline you truly can "do anything you set your mind to do."

13

EXCELLENCE THROUGH HUMOR or LAUGHTER, THINKING & BOOKS

Charlie Jones
P.O. Box 1044
Harrisburg, PA 17108
717/763-1950

Did you know it is possible for someone to look you right in the eye and not hear a word you said? I made this discovery early in life thanks to the help of my six kids. I knew they were not listening because their eyelids would be struggling to stay up. Often I would catch myself wondering why they weren't listening before I finally figured it out that it was my fault. My six kids did not hear a word I said because I had developed a bad habit of talking to people's ears. And although everybody knows that you hear with your ears and you see with your eyes, because I had only been talking to their ears, their eyes decided they had nothing to do so they would close for a while.

If you are going to enjoy excellence in your life, you had

better learn the technique of not only speaking to the ear, but of going for the heart as well. One of the greatest lessons you will ever learn in communication is to go first to the ear with the point, and then to the heart with an illustration. Watching their eyes light up, you know that you have helped them see with their hearts what they have just heard with their ears.

Their lips curl up as they smile in recognition, as you rush back to the ear again. This is the art of successful communication.

To some, however, it is a lost art. Some teachers don't teach because they spend years drilling rules and regulations into the students' ears and not the heart. Some clergymen never touch the hearts of their congregation because they are content to pour proverbs and psalms into the ears. Some managers and sales people never reach their potential because they set dreams and goals that are speaking to the ears, but not the heart. And, yet, there is an answer available to each of us that only a few have employed — humor.

When you come to the realization that most people love to laugh, humor can be used to pave the way to excellence in life's communication with others. Hearing a truth with the ear can be boring, but discovering a truth with the heart produces the warmth of recognition complete with a smile and sometimes even laughter.

As I stated before, once you make a point, you then need a good illustration to help others mentally see what you have said. Have you ever heard the old saying, "You brought it on yourself"? If you're married you probably hear it every day.

Suppose we worked together and you came to me with a problem, perhaps asking for advice. Now suppose I said to you that you deserved it because you brought it on yourself. The problem is that you already know you brought it on yourself, and I already know you know you brought it on yourself. Do you think I'm going to tell you that you brought it on yourself? No. Why? Because I know how it sounds and I don't like it either.

Sometimes you'll hear someone take pride in the fact that

they "tell them to their faces like it is." That's when I have to say, "You can go to work for our competition. We don't need you around here." If you are going to confront someone with something directly to their face you know you are also involving their feelings and that you'd better go to their heart and help them see it, and not simply hear it.

Like most people, I like to see where I'm wrong or where I'm about to make a mistake. The constructive criticism of others can save us valuable dollars and time. But to like to actually hear that you're wrong is entirely another matter. If I approached you, pointed the finger and said, "you brought it on yourself," there would be a confrontation. We have seen this happen hundreds of times in our day-to-day lives. When confronted, your mind automatically says, "I don't have to take this! I'm going to ignore you." You would become defensive and maybe even want to fight. If, however, you are seeking excellence, the key will not be found in pointing the finger, but rather will be helping others see where they are wrong with a genuine concern and a good laugh, and how they can do something about it. Here is what I mean:

Every day Pat and Mike sit down to eat their lunch. While Mike would quietly begin to eat his sandwiches, every day Pat would go through the same thing. Opening his lunch, he would take a quick glance, and begin to scream, "Oh No! Not this again! PEANUT BUTTER SANDWICHES! I hate peanut butter sandwiches!" Each day Pat was louder and wilder. Finally Mike couldn't take it any more. He yelled over Pat's ranting, "If you hate peanut butter sandwiches so much, why don't you tell your wife you don't like peanut butter sandwiches?" Grabbing Mike by the throat, Pat yelled back, "YOU LEAVE MY WIFE OUT OF THIS! I PACK MY OWN LUNCH!" You may think this is humorous now, but wait until next week when you find yourself eating some of your peanut butter sandwiches again!

Now I would like to share with you the greatest idea you will ever hear. How would you like an idea that will guarantee you'll never hear another poor speaker as long as you live; you'll never hear another dry lecture as long as you live; you'll never hear another dry sermon as long as you live? Wouldn't you like an idea like that? Like so many others, all my life I had sat through countless meetings, conferences, workshops and all I've heard is LISTEN, LISTEN, LISTEN. Unfortunately, the more I listened, the more confused I became. Finally, I caught on. I wasn't supposed to listen—I was supposed to THINK.

There is a world of difference between listening and thinking, between memorizing and realizing, between listening to a great speaker by memorizing and improving yourself simply to project a better image, and actually thinking with speakers as you realize and become better without actually trying to be better. So what should we be trying to do? A few simple changes in our daily routine can improve the quality of our lives. From now on when you read a book, hear a speaker, or listen to a sermon, always take your pen. As you get used to reading or listening with a pen in your hand, you begin to cultivate the habit of making notes of things you actually think rather than what you thought you heard. We must learn to listen, but only enough to get our own minds in motion and start our individual thought processes. I try to practice this in church. When the pastor starts to preach, I take out my pen and start making notes of things I think. This excites the pastor because he thinks I'm writing out his sermon. Sometimes I think he should throw away his sermon and use my notes. As I leave church I get a smile or laugh when I say, "Pastor, you were really good this morning. You interrupted my train of thought a half dozen times." Whether it is selling, preaching, or teaching, interrupting the train of thought to help them see what they know will always bring a smile or a laugh.

The highest compliment you can pay me is to say, "Charlie, I don't remember a word you said, but I can't remember a time when I so enjoyed laughing at my problems and seeing more clearly things I already knew." Sometimes I'll hear, "You talk so fast I can't remember what you were saying." That's why I talk fast, because when you leave my meeting at least you're going to leave even. One of my objectives in communication is stimulating the mind to think by a rapid bombardment of old truths. There are many factors that can lead to excellence, but none more important than humor; and that's why one of life's greatest discoveries is thinking.

Everyone who knows me knows my trademark is books. As a salesman it was books; as a manager it was books; in my home it's books; in my friends' lives it's books. Years ago I had a habit of giving everybody a book. I hoped they were read, but if not, they were there to be read.

Some time ago I attended a lecture. I don't remember much of what the speaker said, but he had me laugh for an hour at my problems as I identified with many principles that convinced me that even though we had never met we were very much alike. As he closed his talk he said, "You are the same today that you will be five years from now except for two things — the people you meet and the books you read." If you hang around achievers, you will be a better achiever; hang around thinkers and you will be a better thinker; hang around givers and you will be a better giver; but hand around a bunch of thumb-sucking complaining boneheads, and you will be a better thumb-sucking complaining bonehead.

The trouble with our heros is that we can't take them home. We have got to grow and experience the lessons of life alone. Aloneness versus loneliness. Some people think they're lonely because they're young, while some people think they're lonely because they're old. Some people think they're lonely because they're poor, and yet some people think they're lonely because they're rich. Some discover that everybody is lonely to some degree and that's the way it's supposed to be. You discover out of loneliness comes aloneness when you decide to live and grow. You alone decide to live your life and do your growing. No woman grows for a man. No man grows for a woman. No parent grows for a child. When you grow, you grow alone. Growing brings growing pains but the laughs come too if humor is a part of your growing.

General Patton made his troops mad and glad. He made them think and laugh when he wasn't around. General Patton once said, "If we're all thinking alike, somebody isn't thinking." When you're thinking, you're constantly discovering new dimensions to everything; when you're the wisest you know the least; and when you're aware of your ignorance, you're the wisest. How good it is to realize my ignorance. General Patton said not to be afraid of fear, "Fear is like taking a cold shower. When the water is ice cold, don't tip-toe in—leap in and spread the pain around. Success isn't how high you reach success is how high you bounce every day when you hit the bottom." Patton almost always helped his listeners see with their hearts what he was saying.

Abraham Lincoln is the most revered name in the world today. No name is so loved and respected as Abraham Lincoln. Lincoln had little education, and yet many people will tell you that the secret of excellence is education. Many believe if you're raised in a ghetto or a broken home you don't have much of a chance. He didn't have a door in his cabin; in fact, the year after his mother died there were eight people in that one-room cabin.

There's a lot of emphasis on self-esteem today and Lincoln had none. But what about self-image? I worked with Dr. Maltz for years, the author of the best seller, *Psychocybernetics*. He helped me to appreciate a good self-image. Lincoln was short in this area, too. His mother died when he was a boy. He never had much time with his hard working father. His sister died when she was in her teens. The first girl he loved died. The woman he did marry didn't make his life a bowl of cherries.

Do you wonder how a man who lacked everything that we say you should have could become the most revered name in the world? Two of the many great assets of Lincoln was his ability to tell stories in order to illustrate a point and then get people to laugh with him. Most of this was stored in his mind and heart with the books he read as a boy. Lincoln was a great thinker because he learned to read and to laugh.

I would be remiss if I talked about excellence and my philosophy if I didn't mention Oswald Chambers. Every word I have spoken for 30 years has been flavored by this man. And it's no small wonder that many have never heard this name because Chambers died in 1917 at age 43. He never wrote a book. Well, how can I have thirty of his books yet he never wrote a book? He married the Prime Minister of England's secretary and when he went to work with the YMCA in Egypt, she went with him and made shorthand notes of his talks. When he died in 1917, she lived on for years and wrote all the books from the notes she'd made. Let me tell you why I love Chambers. He's my favorite writer who helps me see how wrong I am. Chambers says, "You can determine how lazy you are by how much inspiration and motivation you need to do something. If you're for real, you do it whether you feel like it or not. The best way to avoid work is to talk about it."

Get people to think with you and you'll get them thinking better. Get them laughing, but don't let them laugh at you. Comedians get paid to get people to laugh at them. Good managers, teachers, and sales people learn how to get people to laugh at themselves.

I urge you to read and motivate others to read. Never read to be smart, read to be real; never read to memorize, read to realize. And never read in order to learn more, as much as you read to re-evaluate what you already know. Never read a lot, but read just enough to keep hungry and curious, getting younger as you get older.

The heart of excellence is one word for me — thankfulness, learning to be thankful. The first mark of greatness is thankfulness; the first sign of smallness is thanklessness. An attitude of gratitude flavors everything you do. Once in a while some young tiger will say to me, "Did you feel this way years ago when you didn't have anything?" I used to go home and say, "Honey, look at me, 'Man of the Month.'" Look at this, "Man of the Year." She would say, "Where's the cash?" I'd say, "Honey, if we don't start learning to be happy when we have nothing, we won't be happy when we have everything." Well, I never sold her, but I finally bought it myself. I'm not trying to sell you, I'm buying it myself and sharing it. The one great thought, more than any other, is to be more grateful and thankful. When my family sits down to eat, our giving thanks goes something like this, "Dear God, we thank you for our food, but if we had no food we would want to thank you just the same. Because, God, we want you to know we're not thankful for just what you give us, we're thankful most of all for the privilege of just learning to be thankful." Thank you for reading my thoughts. I hope you were thinking with me and that someday we'll meet and you'll tell me I interrupted your train of thought several times.

14

TAKE CHARGE OF YOUR FUTURE

Patricia Fripp
527 Hugo Street
San Francisco, CA 94122
800/634-3035
800/553-6556 (in CA)

Have you seen the commercial where Angela Lansbury is talking about her credit card? She says, "I don't want a credit card that impresses; I want a credit card that gives me possibilities." Business today is full of possibilities. We need, therefore, to be effective communicators. I am frequently asked if I get nervous before I speak to a large audience. Of course, there are times that I am, but I feel very strongly that our value in the marketplace depends very much on how easy or how difficult it is to replace us. If we learn to stand up and speak eloquently with confidence – in fact, if we can stagger to our feet and say anything at all – we'll be head and shoulders above our competition, no matter what we do. We have to learn to communicate effectively to be successful today.

Professor Albert Mehrabian studied communications at UCLA for 20 years and he wrote a book called *Silent Messages*. He said, "When it comes to developing trust and believability, which is certainly what you need in business, seven percent is what you say, 38% is how you say it, and 55% is how you look." That isn't how you dress; it's body language and facial expressions. No matter what words you use, no matter how eloquent you are, people can tell if you're sincere.

One of my best friends in San Francisco is a man named Bert Decker. He is the founder of Decker Communications, but years ago he was a filmmaker. He once had the opportunity to bid on a job that was worth $250,000 a year to his company. Forty people were given the opportunity to bid on the job with written proposals, but only three were invited in for an interview. Bert had a friend on the committee that said, "Your proposal is the best; don't worry." But after the interview, he didn't get the job. Bert asked, "How come? You told me my proposal was the best." His friend said, "Bert, it was, but in the interview you looked nervous. People will not give a quarter of a million dollar project to a person who looks nervous. People will not believe you if you look nervous; people will not be led by you if you look nervous." Be an effective communicator.

The first time Reagan debated Carter some political consultants gathered some high-powered CEO's and asked them to watch the debate and tell them afterwards how they felt about the issues (they stressed the issues!). When they gathered together again one executive said, "I liked the way Reagan shook hands." Another, "Carter didn't appear to be presidential." And yet another, "I liked the way Reagan chided Carter and said, 'There you go again, Mr. President.'" Nothing to do with the issues — all to do with communication skills.

A young man that worked for me got his dream job in Indianapolis working for a rock-and-roll promoter. While in my employment, I sent him through the Dale Carnegie class, so he really felt comfortable standing up and speaking. As the newest employee of his new firm, he was called in to his boss's office one day. The boss handed him some papers and said, "Read it. Do you understand it? Tell me what you think it says in your own words. Now, get on an airplane at four o'clock this afternoon and fly to West Virginia and give a presentation on our point of view at our industry meeting." Don't you think this young man has a better opportunity to be promoted in his company? The boss had more confidence in sending him to give the speech than anybody else, even himself!

John Molloy in *Live For Success* reports that only 20% of people graduating from college today can give a halfway decent verbal presentation, while leading marriage counselors say that 50% of all divorces are caused by poor communications. Peter Drucker, management expert, says that 60% of all management problems are caused by poor communications. As Ralph Waldo Emerson said, "It's a luxury to be understood."

I started my working career at age 15 as a hairdresser in England. My father paid $250 for me to go to work for $4.50 per week. It wasn't one of the most affluent times in my life! But, at that point, two people were sowing some seeds I fortunately had enough sense to listen to and that I've tried to use all my business life. I saw my first boss, Mr. Paul, treat every woman that came in the salon like she was the only one in the world for the amount of time that she was there. My father, who became a very successful real estate businessman, always said to me, "Don't concentrate on making a lot of money; concentrate on becoming the type of person that people want to do business with and you most likely *will* make a lot of money."

Isn't that really a key point in business today? As business becomes more competitive, it should be more fun, more efficient and more professional to do business with us rather than our competition.

One of my clients, Fantastic Sam, who owns the haircutting franchises, told me he has a notice on the wall of his office saying, "God is watching; give Him a good show." He said, "I'm not a particularly religious person, but having that plaque on my wall makes it easier to make business decisions." I ask you, if you had a sign in your office saying, "God is watching; give Him/Her a good show," would you do anything differently? It's a good philosophy to take to work. The important thing in having a philosophy is that it helps you through the frustrating times we all experience, because you know what your purpose is and why you're turning up every day and how you want to run your business.

Certainly a lot has changed since I went to work well over 20 years ago. The economy is changing; the business climate is changing; the work force is changing. In the 1950's 70% of American families were traditional. That number has now been reduced to about nine percent. Today 51% of the workforce is women. According to Roger Blackwell of Ohio State, 52% of the people in college today are women. The fastest growing segment in college today is the 25-40 year old woman. Today, more jobs are being created by entrepreneurial ventures than by corporations. Fifty-one percent of all the products available by the year 2000 have not been discovered. Forty-one firms on the Forbes 100 list in 1945 had disappeared by the year 1977. Many of the companies on today's Fortune 400 list didn't exist in 1920. Even the relationship between men and women is changing. Gloria Steinam said, "Women today are becoming the men they used to want to marry." She added, "Men are not becoming the women they used to want to marry, so who's doing the washing up? I don't know."

Even people's attitudes are changing. Older people are getting more optimistic, younger people more pessimistic. I don't know how you feel about changes that are happening in the world we live in, but many people I talk to are very nervous about change. I would like to suggest to you change is inevitable and there are three things you should think about in terms of change: 1) Change is good and necessary. 2) Cultivate a desire to participate in change. 3) Believe you can make a difference.

There are two ways you can react to change: from intelligence or from necessity. The intelligent way is to think, plan and organize how you want your life and future to look. If you react from necessity, other people are controlling your future. I realize that when I ask you to think, that's easier said than done. Leo Rosten said, "Thinking is harder work than hard work." Surely, our value to ourselves, our families and our organizations is in the fact that we can think. Yet 72% of managers who replied to Alex McKenzie's time survey said they didn't have time to think or plan—surely our number one priority.

I'm not so naive as to think I can give you a simple formula for how you can take charge of your future in changing times. But I will suggest, if you are going to be in charge of that future, there are three ingredients you need: 1) A good sense of direction. 2) A good, healthy body (it's difficult to be a dynamic success if you don't feel well.) About 80% of diseases today are lifestyle induced. 3) A good support system. Leaders get results through people.

Let's look at a good sense of direction. I think planning is focusing on the preferable future rather than the probable future that comes about if you *don't* plan. It doesn't mean your career or future will work out exactly the way you plan, but it's the process of thinking that's so important. Recently in San Francisco, I addressed an organization called Women Entrepreneurs. I asked them, "How many of you have had something happen in your career that you considered at the time somewhat devastating?" Everyone put their hand up; some put up two. When you plan, you don't plan for the bad things to happen, but things do go wrong.

I promise you that when you look back at all the setbacks that happened in your career and you take an overall picture of the tapestry of your life, these terrible things will, at most, appear inconvenient. Not devastating—inconvenient.

I've had some wonderful business, a great staff and yet inconvenient things have happened. I've had staff that quit at inopportune moments. I've had people disappoint me. I have been embezzled. When I look back, at most it was inconvenient. I truly believe that I serve my clients better today, not necessarily because of the successes I've had, but because of my ability to adapt to the inconveniences. I'm sure you'll find the same is true for you.

Think about the way you want things to be. I always

wanted to grow up and be successful. When I was a 15-year-old shampoo girl in a chic salon in England, we had all these glamorous rich customers. As soon as I got to know them I'd say, "What were you doing when you were my age? How did you make your money? Did you make it yourself or did you marry it?" You may think that was being nosey but I considered it good market research!

All my life I figured this was the way to be successful — find out how people planned their futures. One of the most successful women I met in my hairstyling salon in San Francisco is a speaker and consultant named Dru Scott who wrote, *How To Put More Time In Your Life*. She always seemed calm and never raced around frantic like me. One day after she'd had her hair done and I'd given her a cup of coffee, I said, "Sit down, Dru. Tell me, how did you get what you want?" She said, "Patricia, it's really rather simple." (I don't know about you, but when I meet people and they say, "Yes, I'm successful, but it was outrageously complicated," I'm less likely to take notes than if somebody says, "It's very simple.") She said, "All I do actively on a daily basis is look after each area of my life. Every day I do something nice for a friend. I drop a note of appreciation or call and say hello. Every day I do something nice for me, even if it's only soaking in a bubblebath for 15 minutes without feeling guilty. Every day I do something for my mind by reading or listening to cassettes."

I was presenting a series of programs for AT&T in Morristown, New Jersey. One of their researchers from the company who followed me on the program said, "All the knowledge we have in the world right now is going to double in the next two years." That means if you have the same job in the same community, you would have to change just to stay the same. I challenge you to think about what time you invest, on a regular basis, not only in keeping up with your industry, but keeping up with the world you live in.

Dru said, "Every day I do something for my body. I run or exercise." It's very difficult to be a dynamic success if you don't feel well. A new Gallop Poll survey shows that the number of Americans exercising has jumped to a full 69%.

Exercise also seems to be a motivator for people to change their health habits and their diets. In a new survey, 64% of the exercisers have started eating a healthier diet compared to 47% of non-exercisers. And 43% of them have lost weight versus 31% of sedentary people. Another key point is that 19% of the population feel very strongly that they are well satisfied with life. But for the health conscious, that percentage is twice that of the general population — 40%!

But life and health consist of more than moving your body and eating vegetables. We are realizing that a positive mental attitude, a feeling of control over life, is essential to mental and physical well-being. The cornerstone of intelligent optimism is the certainty that you have the power to protect your most important resources — a good mind in a fit body. As management expert Peter Drucker says, "We view health as the capacity to manage ourselves to be at our best."

Dru continued, "Every day I do something to keep in touch with the people that now do business with me. Every day I do something to get in touch with somebody who doesn't do business with me now but could in the future. Every day I pray; every day I meditate." What she consciously does, and what I've been aware of since we had this conversation, is to keep balance in her everyday life. We all know that isn't easy because we have pressures. We have time commitments very often beyond our control.

I ask you to think about that every day. Are you leading a balanced life? Are you getting feedback and rewards, not only from business, but your life outside work? A balanced person will make a better leader for the future.

I race around like many speakers and give talks on setting goals, planning and thinking about what you want and many people say, "Patricia, we understand all that stuff; making challenging goals and writing them down, but how do you know what you want?" I say, if you don't know specifically what you want from your life and your career, don't panic. You're probably like most people. But, what I would encourage you to do is think about everything you don't want and work backwards. It's amazing how clear what you do want will appear. If you looked exactly the way you do right now in one year's time, would you celebrate? If not, what are you going to do? If the quality of your relationships is exactly the same, in and out of business, in one year's time, would that be marvelous? If not, what communication skills are you going to have to learn or use? What time are you going to have to take with the people you think are important to you? If your career took the same natural progression as it's taking right now, is that wonderful? If not, what are you going to have to do? What are you going to have to learn? What will you do to change the future?

There's an old story about a man that was fishing. Every time he caught a fish he'd measure it. The little ones he'd put in the pail and the ones 10 inches or longer would be thrown back in the lake. There was a man further along the bank watching him and he thought that this was rather peculiar. He went up to the old man and said, "Excuse me sir. Why are you throwing away the biggest and best fish?" The old man said, "I only have a nine inch frying pan." Isn't that like life? Very often when we sit down and project the future, we set goals or make plans and then we think, "Oh, that's not possible. I don't have enough help. I'm not smart enough. There's not time enough in the day." Somebody should have told that man all he had to do was cut the 12 inch fish into one inch pieces then they'd fit in his nine inch frying pan. That's what we have to do with the challenging plans we dream about in the future. What "piece" are you committed to each and every day?

I say to people, "Tell me what you say you want and show me one week of your life. I'll tell you with 98% accuracy whether you'll get it." I have a bunch of cronies that I get together with for lunch every few months. Now, to me, a crony is one up from a friend. These particular cronies I met in a Dale Carnegie course about 12 years ago. We meet to commit our goals to each other and follow up on each others' progress. One of my friends, Jim, has been saying for several years that he wants to trek through the Himalayas for his health goal. I keep telling him he can't write it down because he doesn't even backpack today. If he writes that as one of his goals, it will totally invalidate everything he wants in his business and life because he's not doing anything *now* to get closer to it.

Speaker Danny Cox says the difference between a goal and a fantasy is that you know something that you can do tomorrow to get closer to a goal. A fantasy is something you just sit in the bubblebath and enjoy. There's an important place in life for both goals and fantasies but don't confuse the two. As Ken Blanchard, author of *The One Minute Manager*, asks, "Are you interested in or committed to your plans and goals? If you have an interest in what you're doing you do what you have to do. If you have a commitment to your goal, you never ask yourself the questions "Do I feel like doing it today? Am I in the mood?" or "Are the stars aligned?"

What are you committed to every day? More important, you really have to ask yourself what am I committed to do every day even when *I don't feel like it*? What happens a week from Thursday when you're dressed for success and racing out the door and your child throws up all over you? How committed are you to your goals and plans for a bright future when real life sets in? The super achievers never ask themselves the question, "Do I feel like it today?" The superachievers concentrate so much on the results they want they don't even ask the question. Whereas, the mediocre people that just get by concentrate on, "How can I get through the day as comfortably as possible?" If you'll look back through your life, you'll note that most of the results you've achieved have come from being uncomfortable rather than comfortable.

So think about what you want. If you don't know exactly what it is, think about everything you don't want and work backwards. Think about what you have to do every day to get closer to your goal, even when you don't feel like it.

You are responsible not only for motivating yourself but for motivating other people — selling your company's vision to the whole community. You have to be constantly involved in public relations. I know when Dru Scott was talking about getting in touch with people that could do business with her in the future, she was talking about having high visibility in the business community. In business today we have to encourage our people to keep in touch with the people that now give us business. It seems to me that many sales and business people think it's our customers' and clients' job to remember us. I think it's our responsibility to never give them the opportunity to forget us.

I bought my first building in San Francisco from a realtor friend. I kept it for several years then I called him up and asked him to find me another building. I wanted to trade up because I had a lot of equity in my current one. A couple months went by and I didn't hear from him. I called him again and said, "Al, I'm really serious. I want to trade my building." He said, "Okay, Trish, I'll get back to you." I said, "Al, I need you or someone in your office to call me at least once a week so I know I'm on your mind. I have two people a day I meet that are in the real estate business that would love to do business with me." Three months later, without one phone call from Al, I bought a building through someone else.

I've always been a believer in the value of a handwritten note to thank clients for the opportunity to do business with them. Long time sales trainer, Bill Gove, when he was with the 3M Company, used to write notes. Someone was teasing him one day and said, "All you do is write notes all day long." He said, "No, seven minutes a day. Everyone that does business with me hears from me at least once every three months while my competition is calling on them asking them for their business."

In 1969 I worked for Jay Sebring, who was an innovator in men's hairstyling. He got his reputation by doing many of the movie stars — Paul Newman, Steve McQueen and Peter Lawford, to name a few. Jay said a very simple thing that I think about every day in my business life even though I'm in a totally different business. He said, "We only have one gimmick. The best haircut in town." But it wasn't what he said that I found so fascinating — it was who he said it to: *Time Magazine*, *Newsweek* and *Playboy*. This was in 1965 when no one else was talking about men's hairstyling.

Ralph Waldo Emerson said, "If you build a better mousetrap, even though you may live in the center of a jungle, people will beat a path to your door." Not true. You can be the best speaker, the best hairstylist, the best financial institution, but if the world doesn't know about you, you'll starve to death. I realized in 1969 that:

☆ People do business with people they know.

☆ People do business with people that do business with them.

☆ People do business with people their friends talk about.

☆ People do business with people they read about.

I knew to be successful I had to have high visibility so I went on many radio and television shows. I was interviewed by all the local magazines and newspapers. I was asked to do an article on marriage. Obviously, as a single person, I can't be an expert on marriage, but I'm a great observer of human behavior. Several years ago I was invited to speak at a large Possibility Thinking conference at the Crystal Cathedral. I was following Arvella Schuller, a very dynamic speaker, and producer of Dr. Schuller's television show. Arvella told about a conversation she'd had with a marriage counselor. She said to him, "Do you hear hundreds of problems in marriages or does everyone have the same few problems?" He said, "Basically I could sum up all the problems I've heard into two categories: either selfishness or immaturity." He went on to tell her about a couple that came to him for counseling. The wife had told him, "The only thing I ask for in my marriage is to be treated as well as our family poodle. My husband comes home in the evening and pets the dog and talks to him. All I want is a touch and a kind word." Her husband said, "When I come home in the evening the poodle runs to greet me and wags his tail!"

The saddest thing about standing behind a hairstyling chair, which I did for 24 years, is not the varicose veins or sore feet, but the amount of times my customers said to me, "You know, my father died last week or my sister died last week or my best friend died last week . . . and I never told them I loved them." It has been said that if the end of the world was coming in 10 minutes, every phone booth in America would be full. I say why wait? The feelings we have for other people mean absolutely nothing to them unless they know. That's certainly true of your support system at home. It's also true of your support system at work—the people that help you accomplish your goals.

How do you get results through people? First of all you have to understand what motivates them. Why do people work? For one thing, people work to make a living. You can't get too motivated if you don't make the house payment. But beyond that I think that people work as an education. The more they understand about how their job fits into the overall schemes and plans of the organization and its future, the more interesting it is to them. People work for the intrinsic pleasure of doing a good job so they've got to know how they're doing. They've got to get feedback. People work to participate in an event with other people. It's nice to be part of a team. It's very nice to be part of a winning team.

People usually start out in a state of excitement with hope that this is going to be a great job with a great future. A job where they're going to learn a lot, work with great people and serve the community. That excitement can last from half a day to forever, depending on their own personal motivation, the environment and the leadership in that job. The next level they go through is reality, and it's important to be in reality. In real life you have to do what you have to do every day—even if you don't feel like it. In real life it doesn't matter how much money you make, the government takes more than you figured. In real life it doesn't matter how much you like that job, some days you'd rather go shopping or fishing. And, in real life it doesn't matter how wonderful those people are that you work with, sometimes they're a pain in the neck.

What we have to do as leaders is not only create an environment where people function in reality, but we have to create enough excitement in that everyday reality so that they don't get into the next stage. It's called looking. That doesn't necessarily mean looking for another job, but it does mean not being committed to the one they have right now. The trouble with life is that reality doesn't live up to expectations. As Oscar Wilde said, "The bride's second disappointment is Niagara Falls."

To get results through people you have to learn to be a leader. Six good words to learn are, "I admit I made a mistake." Let me tell you why I think that's important. In changing times many of the procedures we use are changing so fast that we're doing them for the first time. It's very difficult for anyone to do something perfectly the first time they do it. If somebody makes a mistake, the important thing is to let them know before it becomes an overwhelming problem. That means they have to realize it's okay to make a mistake, as long as they tell us.

Several years ago I still owned my hairstyling salon while I was promoting myself as a speaker. I needed to hire a new receptionist, someone who was going to manage the shop and greet people, someone who was very high energy. I was looking for the perfect person to give a good first impression of my shop, so I wasn't going to be my usual impatient self. I was going to do the job right this time. I ran an ad in the paper and had 140 calls in a day and a half. I interviewed the best 30 and when it came down to the top four, I had their handwriting analyzed. I had MY handwriting analyzed. I was going to build the perfect team. I made my decision and hired my perfect person. Two weeks later I fired her. I said, "Marta, I'm not saying you *are* miserable but you look miserable. You can't work for a motivational speaker and *look* miserable. It's bad for business!" I also admit to you that 13 years ago I would have kept her in the wrong job for months and justified why I made that decision. The rest of the staff might have quit but I would have had the satisfaction that I was right.

My friends say to me, "Patricia, you're always so positive, even when you're wrong." It's true. But the difference is, show me I'm wrong and I waste no time defending my former position. It's a waste of time. Why do people NOT tell us the truth? They won't tell us the truth because they think they will be negatively rewarded for giving that information. It starts out when we're little children. "Jimmy, did you knock over the milk?" "Yes mommy." Wham! "Jimmy, did you knock over the cereal?" "Yes mommy." Wham! "Jimmy, did you make a mess in your bedroom?" "No, that was the cat." Jimmy grows up and works with people like you and me.

Imagine if I called one of my suppliers, "Mr. Smith, this is Miss Fripp. Where are my widgets? I expected them yesterday." "Hold on Miss Fripp, I'll check with the warehouse. Jimmy, what happened to Miss Fripp's widgets?" "I put them on the truck myself last Thursday." "Okay. Miss Fripp you should get them by today. They went out last Thursday." Does Jimmy ship them out late or pretend they got lost? Wouldn't it be better if Jimmy felt he worked in an environment where he could say, "Hey boss, I messed up. I forgot to write it down." The boss could then say, "Miss Fripp, you are a valued client and we had a mix-up at the warehouse. What can we do to straighten it out?" It's important to create an environment where people will tell the truth.

We have to learn to tell our clients the truth so we can develop good relationships. I got off an airplane at 11 o'clock at night and called for the hotel limo. They said my client had ordered it but since my plane was half an hour late, it had returned to the hotel. I said, "Not a problem, can you send me another?" "I'll try," was the reply. I said, "You don't understand, it's one o'clock in the morning on my time clock. I'm, very tired, either send me a limo or I'll take a taxi but I don't want to have to bill my client for a taxi if you'll send a hotel limo for me." The hotel limo had not arrived after 25 minutes so I called back only to be told, "We never send anyone out after 10:30." The next time I stayed at this hotel a couple of years later, at 3:25 in the afternoon, I was guaranteed the limo would be there in 10 minutes. After waiting 20 minutes I called again. "Another 10 minutes." I waited 50 minutes. When talking to the general manger, I explained my problem was not that they don't send limos after 10:30 at night or not that I had to wait 50 minutes, it was being "10 minuted" to death. The fact that I had fruit, wine and cheese sent to my room did not make up for the fact that I'd have gotten a taxi had I been told I had to wait that long. The note from the general manager did tell me that he absolutely guarantees from now on that every manager, bellperson and desk clerk in that hotel will know exactly what time the limo will be arriving at the airport so they could tell their guests the truth.

The five best words in dealing with people are, "I am proud of you." I'm sure you've read *The One Minute Manager*. It says, "Catch someone doing something right and tell them. And if they don't do it right the first time, catch them doing it partially right and tell them." Thorndyke's Law: "Performance that is rewarded tends to be repeated." I had a young woman work for me about six years ago. Seven years ago she had made the decision "I am an alcoholic. I can't ever drink again." I don't say it was easy living with that resolution, but it was easier, because her support system at home and at work said on a regular basis, "I'm proud of you."

The four best words in dealing with people are, "What is your opinion?" I can tell an awful lot about the organizations I work for, not by meeting the executive-type men or women, but by meeting the people in the organizations that might not be perceived as important. Five years ago I got off an airplane to do a program for what was then the Ohio Bell System. I was looking for an executive man or woman but didn't see anyone that looked like that. So I was walking over to the phone to call my office when I saw a man with a label. He didn't look the way I expected someone that would be greeting me would look. His suit was very shiny, his collar was turned up, his trouser legs were too short. But his label said "Ohio Bell." I thought, well, maybe executives dress like this in Ohio! I said, "Are you looking for me?" He said, "Oh yes, Miss Fripp, I'm looking for you. You're going to love speaking for our people. We have the best group of people who ever worked together anywhere." I replied, "How long have you worked for Ohio Bell?" This enthusiasm sounded like it was his second day. He said, "23 years." I said, "What do you do for Ohio Bell?" He said, "I'm a driver, I drive the executives." For the 45 minutes it took to get to the office he told about his fellow workers. He said, "One man you must meet while you're here is one of our vice presidents. A man named Joe Reed." I asked, "What's so good about Joe Reed?" He replied, "He asks me what I think." That night I was being entertained by two of the secretaries. They said, "Patricia, the way our company is going, we might not have jobs in two years. There might not be secretaries within the Ohio Bell." I said, "That has to make you nervous to think that no matter how hard you work you could end up without a job in two years." They answered, "No, for the experience of working with the quality of people that we're working with, it would be okay if we end up without a job in two years."

Well, I've never had more than 10 or 12 people work for me at once. It's tough making just 12 people feel good all the time. I wanted to find out how on earth this is accomplished in big organizations. I had breakfast with their boss the next day who has been trained by Joe Reed. I said, "What do you do to make the people around here feel this good? "One technique I use," he said, "that seems to work fairly well is that every couple months I sit down with everyone that reports to me and I have a three-on-three session with them. I say, 'What three things do I do in managing you that you like that I should try to do more of?' and 'What three things do I do in managing you that you don't like that I should do less of?'" You understand what that executive was doing was very scary. He was opening himself up for feedback.

If we're open for feedback we are much better as leaders and managers, but it's much better to give it than to get it. I thought this was a great technique; it's not complicated and not only can I talk about it in my seminars, but I can also use it in my own business.

I went back to my staff and said, "I want to be a great leader — one of these people they write books about. If you have any feedback on my almost perfect management style, I want to know." A young woman called Jimmie, who worked for me at the time, said, "Since you asked...Do you realize that when you give me my instructions in the morning you point and I don't like it."

Now, you understand the truth and someone's perception of the truth, might not be exactly the same. After all, I am an energetic, enthusiastic, frankly noisy person. I give speeches and point. It was not my perception that I was shouting and pointing. But at that point in time her perception was more important than mine. So based on that valuable input I never would have received had I not asked, I put my hands behind my back. "Good morning, Jimmie. How are you today? Let's look at your 'to do' pad." And for 10 minutes I would be calm patient, quiet and "un-Frippy." Would I want to live my entire life calm, patient, quiet and un-Frippy? No. But for 10 minutes a day, if that young woman felt better about herself, better about working in my organization that I had more invested in than she did, I could certainly modify my personality—not change. You don't change a personality without going crazy, but you can modify. You might say, "But, Patricia, you were the boss. Let them modify their behavior to you." Nice, unrealistic, but nice.

Michael Korda in his book *Power* talks about two types of power. The position power says you're the boss, you're the president, you're the teacher, you're the parent. The personal power makes people want to help you accomplish your goals. It's nice to have the position power but it won't take you far if you don't have the personal power to go along with it. If you have a secretary in an office typing at seven o'clock at night when nobody knows that he or she is there, I tell you she is doing that for the personal power of the person she works for, not the position power.

Do you realize that people can smile at you and totally sabotage everything you're doing at the same time? Marilyn Manning, speaking on "conflict resolution," tells about a gentleman in Sacramento, California, who had the opinion that women with children shouldn't work. His assistant, however, was a single parent with two children. She had no choice. This was not self-improvement or luxury, this was survival. One afternoon she raced in and said, "I need to leave immediately, my child is in the hospital." He said, "You know the procedure. Type out a request and I'll sign it." She went to her office, typed out a request and came in again. He was talking on the telephone and rather than initial it while he was on the phone he turned his chair around, put his feet up on the window ledge and continued the conversation obviously longer than necessary. He turned back, signed it and she left, but she set a new goal for herself that night. It took her six months to accomplish that goal but that gentleman was not in his job anymore. Develop your personal power.

A manager has to get everybody involved. He has to make them think and think long-term. He has to make them understand that he respects their opinions. A lumber company in the Northwest had a problem. Many of the logs were falling off the assembly line. As a very last resort, the owner of the company said to the men, "Hey guys, you got any ideas on how we can stop these logs from falling off the assembly line?" One quiet little guy spoke up. His name was Charlie and he'd been around for about 20 years. He said, "Well boss, if we tried such and such I bet it would work." They tried it and it worked. It saved the company $1,000 a day.

Well you can imagine that they were rather pleased. They had a banquet to honor Charlie. They gave him a plaque and a check for thinking. All the guys were saying, "Charlie stand up and say a few words." This meek little guy got up, looked around sheepishly and said, "Well, I really appreciate this nice evening, this plaque and the check. It will come in very handy at Christmas. But I don't know why you're making such a big fuss. I thought about the idea five years ago." One thousand dollars a day and he thought about it five years ago! Everyone said, "Well, Charlie, why didn't you tell us?" He said, "I didn't think my job was to tell you what I think. I thought my job was to put the logs back on the assembly line." As leaders, you get results through people. Tap their minds, their creativity and make them feel important.

(Thanks to Boo Bue, Dale Carnegie sponsor, for the above story.)

The Illinois Bell Pay Phone Division used to have no competitors. Now they have 200. They had a "Just Imagine" program and I was there when they were three weeks into it. The program was for the regular employees, not the executives, to get together once a week and brainstorm with other people on how they could save money for their company. Two of the groups had already come up with ideas that would save the company a quarter of a million dollars for each idea.

As chairman of Electronic Data Systems, H. Ross Perot said, "Any company that spends a lot of time on internal fighting will lose the battle against the competition. It's always going to be beaten by a company who operates as a team."

One of my former hairstyling customers, Al Stanton, told me an interesting story. Early in his career he worked in the traffic department of the Zellerbach Paper Company. One of his duties was to handle the travel arrangements for Isador Zellerbach, the founder of the company. Mr. Zellerbach was a very personable man who believed in making all of his employees feel important. Stanton appreciated the fact that Mr. Zellerbach would frequently ask his advice on different matters. One day Mr. Zellerbach told him a story from which we can all learn a great deal.

Early in the history of the company a Zellerbach truck was following a man in a rather fancy car on a narrow road. The truck driver was very impatient to pass and kept honking. After about 15 minutes, when he finally did pass, he put his head out the window and yelled, "You ____, you want to take up the whole road?" Meanwhile, the Zellerbach name was all over the truck!

It happened that the gentleman driving the car was the owner of the company that was Zellerbach's best customer in the area. When he returned to work he stormed into his office and told the purchasing agent to cancel all orders with Zellerbach and never to buy anything from them again.

It was several months before this lost account came to the attention of Mr. Zellerbach. He tried to get the gentleman on the phone and couldn't so Mr. Zellerbach went to speak with

him in person. When he heard the story he was shocked—
shocked that he had overlooked one of the most important
factors in his business. That absolutely everyone, including
the janitor, represented his company. So, from that point on,
Zellerbach's truck drivers received lessons in politeness and
human relations.

Paul Harvey said, "For a company's advertising strategy to
work it has to be handled not only corporately but also
individually." Individually and collectively companies large
and small spend a fortune promoting their public image. It
only takes one person to ruin that image. Management's
biggest problem is to make everyone in the company understand they play a very important part in the overall schemes
and plans of the company.

A few years ago the National Speakers Association was in
Nashville for a winter workshop. We had a board meeting and
we'd been going on for hours. Six of us adjourned to the
coffee shop to continue our conversation. We were not trying
to be awkward but being speakers we never stopped talking
for a moment while the waitress was taking the order.
Nobody wanted anything exactly as it was presented on the
menu and nobody wanted the same as anybody else, but the
waitress was nice and patient. At the end of ordering I said,
"My dear, this is going to be worth your while. These guys are
big tippers." She said something I've never forgotten. She
said, "I'm not being nice for a tip. I don't care if you don't
give me a tip. I just feel if we give you good service, your
group will come back to our hotel next year." I was impressed. This was a waitress talking about "our" hotel. I went
back to my office and sent a letter to the manager. "Dear Sir:
I am a motivational speaker. I travel nationwide talking about
good and bad service. I would like to commend you. Your
staff was superb but especially this waitress. . ." I related the
tale. I continued, "I don't know what you do to motivate your
people, but keep doing it, it works." I never had a reply. I
think maybe the waitress and the manager should change
places for a couple of weeks! She knows more about public
relations than the manager.

Working together as a team is not easy. Working together if the team does not have a good leader is practically impossible.

The three best words in dealing with people are "If you please." The two best words, "Thank you." And the one best word is "We." How can WE improve service for our clients together?

In changing times you need a good sense of direction. Think about what you want to do. If you don't know exactly what you want, think about everything you don't want. Remember, your number one priority is to think and plan and, at the same time, to get results through people. Appreciate your support system at home and at work. Get them involved. Ask them what they think. Make sure they know it's okay to make a mistake as long as they tell you about it.

Albert Einstein said, "Let us not strive to be people of success, but people of value." For surely, when we are of value to our staff, our community, our industry, our families and each other, then we really will be a success.

15

STOP HOPING AND START COPING

Ira Hayes
326 Meadowlark Ct.
Marco Island, FL 33937
813/394-0830

The huge cat's explosive roar split the calm twilight, and was immediately joined by the man's shriek as the two tumbled onto the dusty plain. The two sounds blended into one chilling chord of struggle; the killer beast rumbling its deadly growl of slaughter, and the man screaming in the terrified determination of defense and survival.

The weight of the massive cat slammed the man onto his back, stunning him and knocking his stone club out of his grip. The beast crouched low over the victim and dropped its jaw for the crushing bite that would snap the man's neck.

From behind the boulders that framed the opening of the man's subterranean dwelling, the women and tiny children stared in silent resignation. Beyond hope, beyond thinking, the trembling figures in the rocks could only leave the man to cope with his fate. To succumb or survive the prehistoric tiger's attack was up to him alone.

The beast lunged at the man's neck and shoulder, but the

wiry victim rocked forward and hugged the tiger's throat against his chest. Beneath the cat's fiercely working jaws, the man held on with a death grip. The gleaming yellow fangs slashed at the empty air and the roaring beast's hot breath poured down the man's naked back. The struggle continued from heartbeat to heartbeat, the caveman taking in every move the tiger made and countering with his own defenses. The big cat and the man tumbled and scrambled together, claws matched against hands, fangs matched against cunning.

Methodical in his panic, resolute in the deadly significance of the match, the caveman's awareness kept up with the split second timing of each movement. The claws continued to shift and slash as the man managed to move the struggle closer and closer to the spot where he was originally seized by the ravenous beast.

One hand left the conflict to dart out to the side and then return immediately to the clash. Again the hand flew out, but this time the fingers felt the familiar worn wooden grip of the stone ax that had saved the man's life so many times. The hand curled around the handle, the arm pulled up and inward, and the stone club sailed up, over, and down onto the back of the tiger's skull. The jolt rocked through the beast's body. Again the club came up and back down onto the sagging head. With a rasping groan, the big cat slumped to the dusty surface of the plain, sliding off the man beneath it.

Staggering to his feet in a daze, the man looked past the limp form of the tiger to the rocks surrounding the entrance to his underground cave. The human forms there raised their arms as though to salute his success. The man turned and moved away as the people from the cave came forward to claim the slain beast. As his breathing pace returned to normal, the man began to forget about the tiger and direct his attention forward, as he had always done before.

Just like the caveman in the story, all of us today find ourselves in situations where we are confronted with a problem that is our own responsibility to take care of. The problem doesn't always threaten to eat us alive if we fail to jump immediately into vigorous action that guarantees a successful outcome, but whether gobbled up whole or merely nibbled into frustration or failure, it is still the classic struggle of the man against the tigers of the world that would overcome him.

My own story does not at first seem quite as dramatic as that of the caveman who resisted becoming the tiger's dinner. But as a young man just starting out in business in the early 50's with a growing family to support, I realized that success or failure was all up to me. I felt I was looking out at the new tigers of a modern age.

In the decades of activity that made up my life from those earlier days, it became increasingly clear to me that "It is almost impossible not to become more successful or happy if we really want to be." Success, whatever it may be defined as for each of us, is simply the natural outcome of our directed intentions and actions. We can count on success if we really want it. And we can recognize and combat today's tigers in their new guises, waiting to catch us and keep us from our goals.

What I may not have realized as a young man starting out was that the contemporary tigers lying in wait to pull people off the path to success are those subtle, insidious character traits that appear to be so harmless, that many of us do not even think to be on guard against their attack. Though some of us may not see them, those tigers are crouched there every day of our lives. Once we can open our eyes and recognize these tigers as the destroyers they are, we are then prepared to design our own weapons to combat and destroy their all-consuming power over us.

In almost all cases, we would have whatever we really want, if it were not for our tendency to succumb to the negative forces of Carelessness, Laziness, Indifference, Forgetfulness and Temptation.

| *Carelessness* | Being inattentive, incautious, unwary, indiscreet, reckless, inaccurate, negligent, thoughtless or inconsiderate. |

Laziness	Having an aversion to work or effort, slow moving, sluggish or inactive.
Indifference	Without concern, not caring, apathetic, a "so what" attitude.
Forgetfulness	Unable to remember or recall, to omit, inability to think of things.
Temptation	Being attracted by the possibility of gratification or advantage, lured into doing something unwise, being led astray from something that needs attention.

Over eons, since the first caveman discovered that the tigers were out to get him, man has faced a continuously evolving series of threats that have adopted ever-more subtle manifestations. Today, the weapons of old are no longer suitable for coping with modern attackers.

The rock, club, hatchet and spear have given way to a new and more powerful set of weapons designed specifically for the tigers of this age. The road to success is made up of single steps, each taken one at a time. Forming and shaping each of the new weapons is likewise a step by step procedure.

In my own life, I discovered eight crucial points that are the counterforces for coping with the five weaknesses that work to destroy our dreams and keep us from our desired success. I found these eight admonitions to be such powerful tools that I had them printed out on individual cards and hung them from the dashboard of my car. Every morning as I look at the card on display, it reminds me to be alert for those weaknesses that would grab me and drag me down. Every Monday morning I flip to the next card and work on the next counteracting force. After eight weeks, it's time to start over again from the beginning.

The eight weapons to counter and cope with the five weaknesses are:

1. DO IT NOW

If the caveman took too long to complete his powerful ax or stone club, he might be destroyed by the first tiger he meets.

Nothing can be accomplished until you begin. So this first card reminds us of the average persons most serious weakness — the great temptation to put things off until later. When embarking on a new and exciting program of self-improvement, this is a most important card. Sit down right now and write down all those things you know you should have done or have promised yourself or someone else you would do. Whenever this card comes up, let it remind you of one of the greatest and most refreshing qualities a person can have, to be able to cope with things as quickly as possible.

2. ORGANIZATION AND APPEARANCE

If the caveman could not find his club when he needed it, it was too late. And just maybe if the wild beast saw the man walking by with his death-dealing ax, they would learn not to attack.

It is my belief from observing hundreds of people that their inability or lack of desire to get organized is responsible for a great majority of failures. It is why otherwise bright people turn out to be mediocre performers and achieve only a small degree of the success they rightfully could achieve. A disorganized desk, car, or way of life leads to confusion, rushing around, agitation, and a poor attitude. Your appearance is also very important. Each time this card comes up, concentrate that week on straightening up your personal things. Take a good look at your clothes, your hair, your self. Remember how you looked the first day on the job? How do you look today?

3. BE CHEERFUL AND OPTIMISTIC

The caveman who is cheerful and happy over last night's victory conveys an important message to other tigers who may have been watching the death of one of their own pack.

No one wants to hear your problems. They have enough

of their own to cope with. In every thought you have, every act you perform, everything you say, you have the choice of being either cheerful and optimistic – or negative and doubtful. I assure you, success is much more quickly attained when you expect it. It indicates to those around you that you are prepared and confident. Your cheerfulness and optimism will usually be returned to you by the other person. This very important card helps set you off from the crowd because today most of the people you meet are not cheerful and optimistic. In fact, it has become almost unfashionable to smile anymore. You will stand out like a star. Few people can say no when they're smiling.

4. MODERATION
    One strong well-built ax on the caveman's shoulder is far more effective than a dozen makeshift sticks in a bundle somewhere in the cave.

    You may be greatly tempted to rush into new ideas and programs at the expense of other things you should be doing. "Moderation" reminds us that great accomplishments are made, objectives are reached, by a well thought out program of activities that can comfortably be done day by day. Moderation – one of the foundation stones in the life of almost every great person.

5. SAY SOMETHING NICE TO EVERYONE YOU MEET
    The roar of the savage beast is terrifying. The purr of the cat by the hearth is comforting.

    Sincere flattery can go a long way, I'm sure you have experienced the glow of satisfaction that comes when others say something nice about you. Share the feeling! What better way to start a meeting or any other contact than by saying something nice. "You have a beautiful office here, Mr. Jones." "That's a beautiful tie you're wearing." Or even, "How very nice to see you!"

6. DRIVE CAREFULLY
    When travelling, the smart caveman would be keenly

aware of his surroundings lest a tiger catch him unprepared or unarmed.

Generally speaking, most salesmen drive considerable distances to cover their sales territories. Accidents are always waiting for you. Especially when you are rushing or mentally reworking an unhappy situation or trying to beat the clock. Every eight weeks when this card comes up, it reminds you: Put on your seat belt! Drive within speed limit! If you're drinking, don't drive! You can't find success in the hospital!

7. *ENTHUSIASM*
The caveman could stand over the vanquished tiger and beat his chest with a shout of victory so all would know of his personal triumph.

Here is one of the most important of all the cards. Millions of words have been written about it. People spend their lives seeking it or asking how to find it. In my own life, I found that you don't just reach out and grab it. You don't get up some morning and say, "I think I'll start being enthusiastic." I believe enthusiasm is attained through personal experience. As you get better organized, things will go more smoothly. You will be more successful and you will experience that wonderful feeling of accomplishment. You'll find you have a better attitude. As this continues, you discover some bright day you really are enthusiastic—about your job, your family, your success. You are coping, not merely hoping.

8. KEEP GOING
Today the stone ax and the fallen tiger. Tomorrow the bow and arrow and the delicious roasted birds. The next day, new and exciting triumphs in the search for a better life.

There are very few people in the world who couldn't be more successful, make more money, or be happier if they really wanted to. Why are so many unable to accomplish this? They can't keep up a program of self-improvement long enough. Anyone can be efficient and do things for seven weeks. Anyone can stay organized and neat in appearance for seven weeks. Anyone can be cheerful and optimistic for seven weeks or say something nice to everyone they meet, anyone can be enthusiastic for seven weeks. But, the eighth week is when you separate yourself from the great mass of people you compete against. Card number eight is "Keep Going." It reminds you to start over again with number one, *"Do It Now!"*

As our society and technology moved forward from the days of cavemen facing tigers, the complexity of coping with daily life continued to multiply. Man against beast is a recognizable conflict in which the only hope is to cope. In modern life, however, confrontations and conflicts are not always so clear-cut. Many times we can be caught in confusion and the hopeless feeling that life is too much to handle and end up relying solely on hope—waiting helplessly for someone to come along and bail us out. We give up our capability to cope, to deal with difficulties in a direct and positive manner, and begin to cling to hope alone.

It is not always easy to cope. Sometimes retreating to hope seems the most comfortable thing to do. I've found, however, that recognizing the tigers and being armed with appropriate weapons to combat them is one positive step towards making daily life an enjoyable experience. Once I discovered this effective eight point system, I was that much closer to being able to stop hoping and start coping. I am sure you will too. Why not start right now with the message on card number one!

 **DO IT NOW!**

 **ORGANIZATION AND APPEARANCE!**

 **BE CHEERFUL AND OPTIMISTIC!**

 **MODERATION!**

 **SAY SOMETHING NICE TO EVERYONE YOU MEET!**

 **DRIVE CAREFULLY!**

 **ENTHUSIASM!**

 **KEEP GOING!**

Organization and Appearance

It is my belief from observing hundreds of people that their inability or lack of desire to get organized is responsible for a great majority of failures. It's why otherwise bright people turn out to be mediocre performers and achieve only a small degree of the success they rightfully could achieve. A disorganized desk, car, or a way of life lead to confusion, rushing around, agitation, a poor attitude, and, most of all, reflects to customers that you're a pretty poor businessman. They question the advisability of doing business with you. Your appearance, your briefcase, your working tools are very important. Each time this card comes up, concentrate during that week in straightening up your personal things. Take a good look at your clothes, your hair, yourself. Remember, how you looked the *first* day on the job. How do you look today?

Do It Now!

Nothing can be accomplished until you begin. So, our first card reminds us of one of the average individual's most serious weaknesses—the great temptation to put things off until later. When embarking on a new and exciting program of self-improvement, this is a most important card. Sit down right now, and write down all those things you know you should have done or have promised yourself or someone else you would do, or something you want to accomplish. Whenever this No. 1 card comes up, let it remind you that one of the greatest and most refreshing qualities of a person, especially in selling, is the realization by the prospect that you are "on the ball." And when you tell him you're going to do something, you really do it.

Moderation

You will be greatly tempted to rush into your new ideas and programs maybe at the expense of other things you should be doing. "Moderation" reminds us that great accomplishments are made, and objectives reached, by a well thought out program of activities that can comfortably be done quietly, day by day. If you take only two photographs of users each day, you'll have nearly sixty the first month. If you send only two pieces of mail to customers each week, in one year more than one hundred customers will hear from you and know you better.

Moderation: one of the foundation stones in the life of almost every great person.

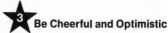

Be Cheerful and Optimistic

No one wants to hear your problems. They have enough of their own. In every thought you have, every act you perform, everything you say, you have the choice of being either cheerful and optimistic—or negative and doubtful. I assure you success is much more quickly attained when you expect it. It indicates to those around you that you are prepared and confident. Your cheerfulness and optimism will usually be returned to you by the other person. This very important card helps set you off from the crowd, because, today, most of the people you meet are not cheerful and optimistic. In fact, it has become almost unfashionable to smile anymore. You'll stand out like a star. Few people can say "No!" while they're smiling.

Drive Carefully

Generally speaking, most salesmen drive considerable distances to cover their sales territories. Accidents are always waiting for you. Especially when you are rushing or mentally reworking an unhappy situation or trying to beat the clock. Every eight weeks when this card comes up, it reminds you: Put on your seat belt! Drive within speed limit! If you're drinking, don't drive! You can't find success in the hospital!

Say Something Nice to Everyone You Meet

Sincere flattery can go a long way. I'm sure you have experienced the glow of satisfaction that comes when others say something nice about you. Share that feeling! What better way of starting a meeting, opening a sales call, or any other contact than by saying something nice.— "You have a beautiful office here, Mr. Jones." "That's a beautiful tie you're wearing." —Or even, "How very nice to see you!" Your objective is to get the order, and I can tell you from my own experience, I've never lost an order complimenting the customer.

Keep Going

There are very few people knocking around the business world who couldn't be more successful, make more money, or be happier if they really wanted to. Why are so many unable to accomplish this? My personal opinion is they can't keep up a program of self-improvement long enough.

Anyone can be efficient and do things for 7 weeks. Anyone can stay organized and neat in appearance for 7 weeks. Anyone can be cheerful and optimistic for 7 weeks—or say something nice to everyone they meet—or drive carefully—or be enthusiastic. But the 8th week is where you separate yourself from the great mass of people you compete with. Card No. 8 —"Keep Going"—reminds you to start again. Here comes No. 1—"Do It Now."

Enthusiasm

Here is one of the most important of all the cards. Millions of words have been written about it. People spend their lives seeking it or asking how to find it. In my own life, I found you don't just reach out and grab it. You don't get up some morning and say, "I think I'll start being enthusiastic." I believe Enthusiasm is attained through personal experience. As you get better organized, things will go more smoothly. You will be more successful and you will experience that wonderful feeling of accomplishment. You will find you have a better attitude. As this continues, you discover some bright day that you really are enthusiastic ... about your job, your family, your success.

16

EXCELLENCE WITH
LESS STRESS

Bill Gove
1-A Atrium Circle
Atlantis, FL 33462
305/964-5225

The late Dr. Hans Selyea did the most research in our society in the area of stress. He defined stress as the non-specific response to any demand made upon the body, suggesting what we already know that it's not what happens to you that does you in, it's not the activating event that burns a hole in your belly — it's how you perceive it, how you respond to it. He has a list of what he calls stressors. Number one is losing a loved one. Number two, surprisingly, is divorce. Apparently the only ones coming out of a divorce looking good are the lawyers. Number three is making some dramatic geographical change in your life like moving in the middle of winter from Pala Alto, California to Dubuque, Iowa. Dropping a bowling ball on your toe was on the list, as was milking a cobra and wrestling an alligator. But, high on the list of the things that keep your life from working was taking yourself, other people and the world around you too seriously.

The last time I was in Dallas I spoke to the Texas funeral directors. They're funny, but they don't know they're funny. They talk about layaway plans. Stuff like that. Did you know, for instance, that when you ship a dead body to another part of the country by air you've got to buy from the airlines for dead Charlie a first class ticket? Now, here's a guy who's been going tourist all his life and now the airlines are asking him if he needs an extra pillow!

I was in Maine recently. Funny people, low keyed. Charlie Gregory sells lobster equipment in the Booth Bay Harbor. Someone asked Charlie how the lobster business was doing. He said, "Monday, I sold a guy some stuff from Pemaquid and Tuesday I didn't sell nothing. On Wednesday the guy from Pemaquid sent all the stuff back. So, I guess you'd have to say that Tuesday was my best day!"

Have you ever heard the term "Idiot Savant?" Well, it refers to someone who is mentally retarded but has highly special- ized skills. There's a sculptor in Boston who is labeled as an Idiot Savant. Yet, I understand he get $1,900 for these little animal figurines that take him about 10 minutes to do. An extraordinary talent who has never spent a day in art school. As a matter of fact, he never spent a day in any school. Another young man has an aptitude for dates. You can give him a date and he can tell you what day it fell on. You would say, "January 25, 1912." He would say, "That fell on a Friday." How about the same date in 2012? He'd say, "That will fall on a Monday." A blind and retarded "Savant" can hear a piano being played and play it back—note for note!

So I asked myself, "What's going on here?" I found out that the average IQ for these three wonderful people was 65. Why, you can't even get into the University of Nevada in Las Vegas with a 65! You can coach there and you can teach there, but you can't get in there!

I thought, "Could it be that what the theologians and the Greek philosophers and the Gurus have been saying down through the years is true after all? That we already have inside of us all we need to be ten times more effective than we already are? Could it be that excellence isn't the exclusive domain of the Edison's and Einsteins and Alexander Graham Bells?

Is it possible, I asked myself, to form the habit of excellence just as you form the habit of sloppiness? I don't know, I can only speak for myself. I've been on the planet for 72 years and I've had some wonderful things happen to me. I have three lovely children and four magnificent grandchildren.

But, I want to tell you something. My big moments, as I look back over my life, have been those times when I was doing something that I loved to do and doing it as well as I could do it. They haven't manufactured the drug yet that will give you that kind of high. Just doing what you're doing, for the doing, not because somebody's looking over you shoulder — not because you're getting an extra bonus. *Just doing it for the doing.*

Nurjev, the dancer, said it for us all when he was a guest on the Merv Griffin Show. Merv said, "It must be wonderful. You dance and they do everything at the end but carry you off on their shoulders." He said, "Interesting, but not important. That's nice but that's not the reason I dance. I dance because I am a dancer. As a matter of fact, once in a while I look over my shoulder to see how I'm doing and I start dancing bad."

Stewart Emory, philosopher, and one of my mentors says this, "At a low level of consciousness a person sweeps the floor for fear of the consequences of not sweeping it. If I don't sweep it, they're going to get on my case. At a high level of consciousness a person sweeps the floor to get it clean."

Isn't this interesting about excellence? Everybody knows what it is. One of the best selling non-fiction books of the last ten years had to do with excellence, *In Search Of Excellence*.

A well-known magazine conducted a study. They asked their readers one question. "What would like to have that you don't have that would make your life work?" As one would expect some of the answers were, "I'd like to have more money, or I'd like to have bigger car, or home or whatever."

However, a surprising number of these readers wrote back and said, "I'd like to get up in the morning and go to a job that I love to do and do it well and at the same time be able to reach out and touch somebody else and make a difference and make my presence felt." We all know what Excellence is, we sometimes don't ask it of ourselves, but we expect and even demand it of others. Our children? Our heroes?

I was in Philadelphia for a meeting and while I was there I went to Veterans Stadium to see the Philadelphia Eagles. If you've ever spent an afternoon at Veterans Stadium, you know what they say about the Philadelphia fans. "The Philadelphia fan," they say, "would boo a cure for cancer." Ron Jaworski, the quarterback, had a couple of sacks and two or three interceptions and the fans were after his blood. They wouldn't get off his case. I looked over to the side and these three people had a big sheet draped over the side of the stadium with a message on it. Now I don't like to be judgmental, I don't know those people and I don't have any right to say anything about them. But, can I say this? They didn't look like Rhodes scholars. Here were people who had settled for so much less than they should have in their lives, but they weren't about to let Mr. Jaworski have the same indulgence. Incidentally, the banner draped over the side read, "We still love you, Ron — signed Mom and Dad!" and the word Dad was crossed out!

I've been asked to consider what I think is the most significant idea I've ever been exposed to. I've thought about it and after 40 years of exposure to new ideas, this is what I consider the best. It has to do with making the distinction between change and transformation. An old Zen analogy goes like this. If you take an apple and turn it into an orange, that's change. You have altered the form. It's no longer an apple, it's an orange. But, if you take an apple and inject something into it and make it taste like an orange, that's transformation because you have transcended the form. It looks like an apple but tastes like an orange.

This suggests that when a person undergoes transformation, that person doesn't change, other people don't change, the world doesn't change. What is altered is the way that person starts to see himself. And other people. And the world.

The word transformation is much more powerful than the word change. I am absolutely persuaded that the secret to living is to transform from a state of being where you spend every waking moment trying to find happiness, satisfaction and fulfillment. When I say I'm satisfied I don't mean that I am satisfied with where I am today. I'm going to keep growing. What I'm saying is, satisfaction is something I do not have to work for! I already have it. It's part of my birthright. I'm entitled to it. I no longer have to strive and try to do things to be happy. I'm already happy. *Then I do things out of that happiness*.

I'm happy *before* I go on the platform and I'm happy after I'm finished, regardless of the audiences response. Let me tell you something. Get this under your skin and the birds will sing for you.

17

EXCELLENCE— AN IDEA WHOSE TIME HAS COME

Ty Boyd
1727 Garden Terrace
Charlotte, NC 28203
800/336-2693

Victor Hugo said a long time ago, "Nothing is so powerful as an idea whose time has come." It was spoken a long time ago, yet it is as powerful today as ever. Some powerful ideas are quite simple. They do not necessarily come through research and development costing millions of dollars.

Someone observed at a recent convention an idea penciled on a no smoking sign. "A Smith and Wesson still beats four of a kind." That is an idea whose time has come. Conrad Hilton was interviewed on television. After an hour program, the interviewer asked Mr. Hilton if he would like to say anything else to the American audience. He replied, "Yes," looked right into the camera and said, "Please put the curtain inside the tub before showering." That is an idea whose time had come! A man in New York was seen carrying a large roll of money. When asked what he did for a living he replied, "I am a sports mechanic. I fix football games and basketball games." That is an idea whose time has come.

Excellence is an idea whose time has come-excellence in the corporate world or in people's personal lives. Excellence is today's buzz word. If there is a word overused today, it is *Excellence*. But it is not overly applied in the lives of men and women. It is a powerful idea, a winning benchmark.

Consider some examples from the world of sports. A baseball player in the major leagues will face the pitcher hundreds of times in a season. He will hit the ball about one in four trips to the plate. If he plays three games, he will probably get three hits in twelve trips to the plate. Consider this: if a baseball player does get one hit in four times at bat, he will earn somewhere between $40,000 and $250,000 per year. But if he can hit that ball one more time in 12, he can earn a million dollars a year. He can become a member of the Baseball Hall of Fame. He could be one of the greatest celebrities of all time, a great hero! The difference between being very good and being excellent!

Compare the true scores of two golfers in the Professional Golfers Association in a recent year. One golfer shot an average of 70.77 strokes per round in that year. He was very good at what he did. He earned about $130,000. A second golfer who entered the same number of tournaments averaged 70.02 strokes per round. There was less than a stroke's difference between the two of them. The second golfer earned a half million dollars in the same year. One golfer was very good, the other was excellent.

Almost a decade ago, a man happened to sit by the great tennis star Martina Navratilova on an airplane. He said, "Lady, I know who you are. You're not as old as the others, you're not as strong as the others, you have not played against all the competition against whom the others have played. Why do you continue to win when most of the others are lost in anonymity?" She replied, "Because I will do *whatever it takes* to win. You see, I hate to lose." That is tough talk. But it describes her dedication to doing whatever it took it win — the be an excellent competitor and athlete.

Former Dallas Cowboys standout quarterback Roger Staubach once made a similar comment. He said that he did whatever it took to win as long as it was legal. What that says to the observer is that it is alright to play hardball, to take off the gloves, to be the best, to seek excellence. Anyone who does not strive for excellence is not being fair to himself/herself. Let's paraphrase a preacher who was once asked in a sermon, "If you were arrested today for being a (pro) at what you do, would there be enough evidence to convict you?" How many people could respond positively to that question?

The message about excellence is equally important for corporations. Corporations must search for the simple truths that result in excellence. Many times people are afraid to use simple truths because they appear mundane, but those individuals and corporations that achieve excellence are the ones who do simple things. A business enterprise must discover ways to bond the synergy of its employees, to make of them Excellence seekers.

There is a story of a man who was caught in flood water up to his neck. A motor boat came by and a man said, "Come on, brother, I'll save you." The victim said, "Don't worry about me, the Lord is going to save me." The water kept rising. The man moved to the second floor of his house. A second motor boat came by and offered help. The man refused the assistance, insisting that the Lord would save him. The water rose and the man moved to the roof. A helicopter came by offering help. The man refused, and soon drowned. Saint Peter let the man through the gates of heaven. The man said, "I am angry. I want to see the Lord." Saint Peter replied, "This is very unusual, but he does have ten minutes. Go right on in." The man said, "Lord, I am very disappointed. I told everyone that you were going to save me. I believed you and you let me drown." The Lord said, "Look, I sent you two motor boats and a helicopter. What do you want?" People often overlook the obvious, simple truths around them.

Here are two boats and a helicopter that can help direct people in search of excellence. The first boat is called *Responsibility*. Responsibility may be the most important secret of all. Excellence comes from what a person does with what he or she learns. Excellence is not knowing everything, it is doing something with what one knows.

A man named Don Toney runs a service station in Charlotte, North Carolina. Ten years ago, Don bought the station where he was working from his boss who was retiring. After that, he and his wife managed to buy a station every year for the next 10 years. Today, they pump over a million gallons of gasoline every month. When asked about the secret of his success Don replied, "I learned a long time ago that Saturday ain't no holiday." What Don Toney did on Saturday and Sunday, in his discretionary time, determined how well he performed Monday through Friday. A person who just works nine to five Monday through Friday will never attain excellence. Saturday ain't no holiday.

There is a popular line that is used frequently: "Ready, aim, fire." Human nature often dictates that we play it safe, cover our loins, be too protective. People want to get more input, learn more, get some more imput before they "aim." They rarely ever "fire" on the projects on which they work. Many of the great companies have learned to say: "Ready, fire, aim." Note that "fire" preceeds "aim." Action is the key. The difference between efficiency and effectiveness is that efficiency means doing the thing right. Effectiveness means doing the right thing right. Excellence means taking responsibility and doing the right thing. People must take responsibility in order to move toward the goal of excellence.

The second boat is called *Versatility*. The great sports figures must have this quality to be truly great. Great corporate managers must be versatile in handling employees and challenges and market trends and the economy. People can develop enormous versatility if they will use the energy that is normally turned inwardly (with concern for self) and direct it outwardly. We must come out of our own comfort zone and then use that energy.

One of my most trusted mentors and friends is Mr. Kopmeyer, "Success Counselor to Millions." He wrote the four volume encyclopedia of self improvement. He gives us three simple concepts that help make people better at what they do. First, successful people make others feel important. They do not view interaction with another person as a contest. They look for ways to make the other person feel special. Kopmeyer says ever man, woman and child on this earth wears a boldly written but invisible sign which reads, "Please make me feel *important*." What a powerful key!!

Next, is the skill to "ask questions." Kopmeyer, in his *Encyclopedia of Self-Improvement*, devotes lesson after lesson to the little word "ask." He says that a person can get anything, have anything, be anything, do anything if he or she asks enough people. (1) Asks the right way, the right question, in the right framework. And, (2) lets others feel important.

Kopmeyers third point is "listen." Excellence requires the formation of new habits sometimes. People who excel must be good *Listeners*. Good listening habits make people more effective in all aspects of their lives. If there were only one skill that we'd recommend to successful managers, salespeople, husbands, wives, etc, it would be to practice the fine *Art of Listening*.

You've read the "two motorboats," now, the "helicoptor" of our message. The third thing that can save people who search for excellence is this: Look at the bestseller list of all non-fiction books. Most of them will be about how corporations or people who are enormously successful feel about what they do. *In Search of Excellence* is a good example. It is a book about how 43 companies feel about their product, their people, their opportunities and their challenges.

All are moving toward Excellence.

A speaker prepared to address an audience of 1700 people. His schedule permitted only three hours sleep before the presentation. After sleeping till the last minute that morning, he called room service for a light breakfast as he prepared to go to the meeting. "This is Boyd, room 2021. Please send some bran flakes with sliced bananas, skim milk and a little cup of black coffee." Before he could reach the shower, there was a knock on the door. "Mr. Boyd, this is Woody with your breakfast. The speaker was surprised! That bellman was dressed in a tan and black uniform, balancing a silver tray over his head. Marching in the room this energetic bellman asked, "Have you seen that sunshine out there this morning?" Woody marched to the window and opened the drapes. And the room was filled with sunshine. The speaker began to feel good about the day. "Mr. Boyd," said Woody, "I looked through every single banana downstairs and I didn't find a single one you would like. So I took the liberty of bringing you some of our red ripe strawberries. And since nobody ever eats red, ripe strawberries with skim milk, I brought you some thick rich cream. And people seem to like the coffee here, so I didn't bring just a cup, I brought you a whole pot full." That was a man who felt good about what he was doing. He could have gotten by with so much less. The speaker related the story to his audience, and the next morning seventeen hundred people called and asked for Woody to serve them breakfast.

Would you say this is the kind of person who is headed for Excellence?

Now, here are five final ideas that will work for individuals or corporations.

First, check your *feedback system*. Get as much feedback from as many different people as possible — customers, fellow workers, prospects, etc. Don't just talk to people who say what is pleasant to hear.

Second, check to see if a *high level of service* is being maintained in your relationships with fellow workers and customers.

Third, establish a greater *quality* in product and service.

Fourth, make sure your business is *customer-driven*. It should respond to the needs of the people for whom it exists.

Fifth, psychologist Abraham Maslow talks about using potential, self-actualization, through several levels of learning. According to Maslow, a worthy objective is to be so exceptionally skilled and practiced that we *perform in an excellent manner without having to even think about how we do a task*. Bobby Knight, the famous Indiana basketball coach says, "I don't want my players to have to think on the court at game time." They think in their practice sessions. Think, think, think. At game time, we want their practice to direct their exceptional play instinctively.

That is moving toward Excellence.

James Michener wrote the following lines, "The masters in the art of living make little distinction between their work and their play, their labor and their leisure, their minds and their bodies, their information and their recreation, their love and their religion." They simply pursue their vision of *Excellence* at whatever they do, leaving others to decide whether they are working or playing. To them, they are always doing both.

That is moving toward Excellence.

And finally, "The clock of time is wound but once, and no one has the power to know just when the hands will stop, at late or early hour. Now is the only time we have. Live, love, toil with a will. Place no faith in tomorrow for the clock may then be still." If it is worth doing, do it now. Today, this week, this year . . . this life "ain't no dress rehearsal!"

That is Excellence, an idea whose time has come.

18

CREATING WINNERS DURING CHANGING TIMES

Dr. Christopher Hegarty
P.O. Box 1152
Novato, CA 94948
415/892-2858

Exceptional executives are both managers and leaders. Managers organize, schedule, budget and administrate. Leaders inspire, create commitment, act as role models and evoke the highest level of commitment and competence possible from subordinates. Exceptional executives both manage and lead. Only highly competent executives can knowingly create winners. The goal of most leaders is to cause people to feel reverence for the leader. Exceptional leaders induce subordinates to feel reverence for themselves. What are the behaviors of a highly competent executive? Here are the essential characteristics of the highly competent executive.

THE TEN COMMANDMENTS
OF LEADERSHIP

I. Be a visionary. Some call these leaders hallucinators, for they "see" possibilities that others ignore. In their minds, they have a picture of what the future can be and they make that into reality. The Wright brothers had a vision of a new world and even though they were ridiculed and faced incredible hardships, they labored and developed that dream until their tiny airplane took off from Kitty Hawk, North Carolina.

Another way winners use visioning is by reliving excellence again and again. By repeating positive experiences in their minds, they revive enthusiasm, awareness and energy. At the same time, they look over failures and release them, never laboring over what went wrong or dwelling on what did not work. Instead, they relive what went right.

Warren Gregory is an excellent manager and leader and yet was not an immediate success in building winners. His secret was focusing on what would work rather than concentrating on serious failures. Beginning as a part-time financial representative, it took him three years to get enough experience and courage to go full-time. He spent the next eight years developing his skills and gradually became more effective. By the end of his 11th year, Gregory had broken every sales record in the organization's history, surpassing the other 4500 representatives of the company.

Because of his success, he was promoted to a first-level management position. In less than a year he failed. The greatest salesman since the beginning of the company was a washout as a manager.

The story doesn't end here for Warren Gregory had an important quality that distinguishes winners, as described below.

II. Have an evolved ego, not a primitive ego. Someone with a primitive ego spends a great deal of time and energy projecting a certain image to the rest of the world, while a person with an evolved ego deals with others in a straightforward way.

Asking for his old job back, Gregory stepped back down to sales representative and became a co-worker with his former subordinates. Spending the next eighteen months traveling around the country interviewing good managers and reading everything he could find on the subject, he discovered the difference between being a doer/producer and being a manager.

Gregory took another risk by asking for his old management job back. The executives who gave him a second chance found their faith to be well-rewarded, for within seven years Gregory exceeded every management record the company had ever set. Out of the 162 divisions, his office moved to first place for total volume and profits. Going through three additional layers of management, he broke every record at those levels as well.

All of this was done because he wanted to learn and be more competent, not because he felt compelled to demonstrate superior ability. Leaders with a highly evolved ego do not need to prove they are always correct.

At the height of his fame, Albert Einstein was asked, "How do you feel knowing so many people are trying to prove you are not right?" Taking a deep breath and thinking for a moment, the great scientist replied slowly, "I have no interest in being right. I'm only concerned with discovering whether I *am* right or not."

III. Be responsible to people, not for them. Effective managers bring out the best in subordinates and give them enough autonomy to do their jobs effectively. Doing this creates trust. Combine that with responsibility and adequate independence and managers will find subordinates investing more of their own ingenuity to get the job done better.

A telephone company used to post daily jobs to installers and then tried putting all the assignments on the board, letting the installers schedule amongst themselves. Productivity doubled. Given with care and responsibility, autonomy benefits both the worker and the organization.

IV. Be decisive, clear and upfront. Clearly seeing their goals, exceptional managers are willing to be misunderstood and disliked, if necessary, to achieve those ends. Believing honesty *is* the best policy, they tell it straight and don't manipulate subordinates. Because they trust their people and are truthful, they earn the trust of others.

V. Cause people to compete and cooperate simultaneously. While spending energy to create a climate of trust and "team" spirit, outstanding leaders also encourage disagreement, for they are developers of people and ideas and choose to foster diversity of thought in their group. Exceptional leaders cause people to disagree so that more ideas are put forth, preventing what Irving Janis calls "Groupthink." Janis found that outstanding leaders would often remove themselves from important discussions and even intentionally place a "devil's advocate" in the group to stimulate more ideas and create an environment of open, unfettered discussion, constantly sharing and questioning.

Warren Gregory broke so many records because he encouraged his group members to be individually excellent and also to share their ideas so the whole team could function more effectively.

Consider wild ducks. As individuals, they are unruly and highly autonomous, not interested in conforming to the group. Yet when they are focused on a team goal, they do it in near-perfect formation because it doubles their range. Exceptional leaders such as Warren Gregory can get their people in formation when needed.

VI. Be a hard worker, not a workaholic. To be a hard worker may mean putting in long hours and lots of energy and such toil can bring joy and excitement through striving to achieve goals by making sacrifices and taking risks. Non-workaholics measure the results of what they are doing against what the cost is, ruthlessly prioritizing their personal and professional lives. The workaholic, on the other hand, uses work as an escape from life and is always scurrying about keeping busy, trying to delude self and others into believing he or she is worthwhile. Instead of moving towards a clear goal as the hard worker is, the workaholic is driven by the fear of failure based on low self-esteem.

VII. Be a life-long student. One of my early bosses worked steadily, trying to continuously improve his techniques. Often he would tell me, "Chris, I just want to get a wee-bit better at my job every day." Because he continued this through a lifetime of work, he became an excellent manager and worker. Some people give up when they see the discrepancy between where they are and where they want to be, telling themselves, "What's the use? I'll never achieve those results and be *that* good." Some of the world's most respected and well-known writers composed only one or two pages a day. In five years alone, however, that would amount to about 3,000 pages. If they had told themselves they had to do 3,000 pages now or else forget it, imagine the loss to the literary world.

Even though outstanding leaders are life-long students, they are not necessarily impressed with educational credentials alone. One manager hired a new employee and told him he liked his people to work from the ground up. Handing the large, industrial broom to the recruit, the boss declared, "Your first assignment will be to sweep the floor." Pulling his hand up over his mouth, the new employee gasped, "You don't understand, I am a Harvard MBA!" "That's right, I forgot. Give me the broom and I'll show you how it's done."

VIII. Do not clone or expect others to do things the "one right way"—your way. Instead, the exceptional manager measures results, not procedures, looking at the quality of the outcome and whether the goals were achieved, even if the methods seemed unorthodox.

IX. Respect feelings. Even when it may not seem practical to do so, an exceptional boss will remember that people respond to the world on the basis of feelings. We may all pretend that we approach problems from a purely rational and analytical procedure, but the reality that a competent boss understands is that subordinates have strong emotional needs which need to be respected, though not catered to. What seems trivial to one person is vital to another. A mail clerk deciding whether to send a letter first or fourth class may experience the same pleasure as a tycoon handling a huge investment. The exceptional leader will listen carefully and without making the decision, help the clerk handle the problem alone next time.

X. Break the distraction addiction. That means anything that keeps us from concentrating when we need to and can include television, mindless chatter and gossip, coffee or snacks, needless phone calls and unnecessary memos. The distraction addiction can be every bit as devastating as an addiction to alcohol, drugs or gambling for in its most severe form it robs us of energy, vitality and relationships. Exceptional managers do not invest themselves in trivial pursuits, but rather put time in quality activities which have a reasonable assurance of return They understand the secret of time management is not to develop some new system, but rather to appreciate and enjoy the benefits right before them.

All indications are that increasingly accelerated change will be a fact of life as we approach the 21st century. Consider just a few of the changes we have witnessed since the 1960's:

1. The assassinations of John Kennedy, Martin Luther King and Robert Kennedy.

2. Men have walked on the moon.

3. Civil rights legislation.

4. Beginning and end of the Vietnam "conflict."

5. Entry of millions of women into the workforce.

6. The rise of Germany, Japan and other nations as for midable economic competitors.

7. Introduction of the personal computer.

8. Biotechnology breakthroughs that will forever alter the genetic codes of all living things.

Some changes have been swifter than others, even approaching exponential proportions. If air travel had advanced as much as computers over the last 15 years, we could take a morning coffee break every day on a Concord, arriving in Paris after 15 minutes with a cost of $3.00 per person. Robotics has shown remarkable advances, as well. In 1986 a robot could replace six production workers for a cost of $1650 while that same type of robot in 2000 will cost less than the cheapest car available.

We have the exciting possibility to create winners in the midst of this change—people who will capture the opportunities before them and gain victories. Here is a five-step process for becoming an exceptional leader.

1. Practice visioning. Every successful executive is vision driven. In order to test your vision for the future, answer the following questions:

A. I expect the future to be

    a. Confusing

    b. Frightening

    c. Exciting

B. The future will be

    a. Somewhat different

    b. Quite different

    c. Vastly different

C. What I expect to be doing in the future is

    a. Pretty much the same as I am doing now

    b. I don't want to think about it

    c. A job radically changed from what I do now

D. When great and sweeping change comes, I see it as

    a. A crisis

    b. Something that will eventually go back to "normal"

    c. A challenge

E. When I think of the future, I feel
   a. Cynical
   b. Fearful
   c. Hopeful

F. When I am in the midst of change, I feel
   a. Powerless
   b. Lost
   c. In control

If you answered "c" to five or six questions, then your "vision" is clear and you get a 20/20 score. If you answered "a" or "b" to two or more questions, you need to reconsider how you view the future.

2. Be a zero-based thinker.

UNLEARN

Look at the word above for a moment. It is one of the most critical words an executive must consider. A great challenge for today's executives is to unlearn behaviors and techniques which have served them well, because they may no longer be productive. We are entering a new age with new demands and different rewards.

Look at everything as if you know nothing. Question every formula and technique. Incompetent leaders hold on to old ways even if it is not effective for them.

3. Recognize the danger of safety. If you are not willing to rock the boat, you may be heading for another Poseidon Adventure. You must be willing to venture into the unknown, for the biggest risk is the unwillingness to take risks. One study of successful managers found they made correct decisions less than half the time. Less successful leaders sometimes make fewer mistakes, but they don't innovate and test new waters.

4. Become and remain well informed and elegantly communicate your value and values to all who impact your future. I've never met an outstanding communicator, but I have met people who work at reducing feebleness. Our country is in the midst of a breakdown of communications. The most frequent cause of stress in families and organizations is a breakdown in communication between well-intentioned people without the skill to avoid the difficulties. Instead of communicating openness and trust, people antagonize and listen *against* each other.

5. Develop and maintain a keen sense of respect for yourself and others. The goal of most leaders is to cause people to feel reverence for the leader. Exceptional leaders induce subordinates to feel reverence for themselves.

Part of this respect includes preserving a sense of balance between the need to make a living and making a life. In the past, the problem had been over-achievers with a lopsided work existence. Now there is a whole new group of people interested in making a life, but not a living. We need to make both a living and a life — and a balance is required between them.

The future is upon us and it promises to bring drastic, unforseen alterations. Executives committed to change, learning and excellence can create winners in a climate of change. We do not owe our people a brighter future, but rather we owe our future brighter people.

What are you doing to be more competent and prepare for the future? The issue isn't can you be an exceptional executive . . . the issue is will you.

Will you?

19

MANAGEMENT TECHNIQUES THAT WORK OR LEADERSHIP IN ACTION!

Allen J. Hurst
Box 58
Winter Park, CO 80482
800/367-4873
303/726-5024 (in CO)

The challenge of excellence makes certain demands on you as a human being and as a business person. It places that responsibility squarely on your shoulders. Whenever I think of excellence and leadership, which I consider to be synonyms, I think of the challenge that we face each day to do something more right than wrong.

How much better do you have to be in the decisions that you make each day? I don't think a whole lot. There are two dimensions of excellence. One is the "Hair's Breadth of Difference," the difference between good and really great. I find that it's really just a very small difference. . . and makes a big difference in results.

The second is "part way success." You're good already or

you wouldn't be reading this book. You're a success "in-wait-ing." You are in the On-Deck Circle, waiting to get to the plate to at least take a swing at it because leaders always take swings. So how much better do you have to be? I think just a hair's breadth.

Let me give you an example. There was a big game hunter who had an absolutely impeccable reputation. He was the epitome of big game hunters. He had an absolutely cracker-jack eye at a hundred yards. He could put the cross hairs on an animal and drop him, making it appear as though the animal just fainted. However, he had never shot an animal, a big one, at less than a hundred yards.

He and a hunting party of three went on safari in India to hunt the Bengal tiger because his trophy room had been denied the Bengal. First morning out of the compound, they drove 20-30 miles. The jungle was so dense that they could drive no farther. One of the men hopped out with his machete and started chopping through the underbrush. As they got into the jungle, they came to a clearing not a hundred yards across, only 30. As they got to the center of the clearing, they heard the pre-kill growl of a tiger over in the brush. All the men except the big game hunter ran back through the cut in the jungle and got to the jeep just as fast as they could. The big game hunter whirled around and shot the tiger, but the tiger wasn't a hundred yards away, he was only 10 yards and closing fast and he only got the gun to his hip. He shot too quickly and missed. He hit the deck on the butt of the gun and got just as close to the ground as he possibly could. Luckily, the overzealous tiger jumped over his head and went into the brambles, giving the hunter just enough time to make it back to the jeep.

They all went back to the compound and had what we call a "10-martini lunch!" After his nap, the big game hunter went outside the compound and found a log. He put some cans on top of it and moved back 10 yards. Because he had a natural skill with the firearm it wasn't long until he could hit every can at 10 yards. He sat them back up and moved back 20, then 40, then 60, then 80 yards . . . and practiced shooting at each distance. By mid-afternoon he was not only the best long shot, he was also the best short shot. As he started back to the compound, what do you think he saw? It was the tiger practicing short jumps.

There are four keys to leadership in management techniques. The first key of excellence and leadership is that I do what is to my intelligent self-interest. Abraham Lincoln demonstrated in all his writings an ability to think through the chaff right through to the grain. For example, Abraham Lincoln is in the courtroom in front of a judge. Earlier that same day he had been in the same courtroom in front of the same judge on the same point of law and had been awarded the verdict as the plaintiff attorney. He is now, in the afternoon, representing the opposite side of the issue as the defense attorney.

The judge stops the proceeding, calls him to the bench and says, "Mr. Lincoln, I'm confused. How can you be so sure this afternoon, when this morning you were equally sure on the other side of the same issue?"

Mr. Lincoln said, "Your honor, this morning I may have been wrong but this afternoon I know I'm right."

That's the ability to think through to what is to your intelligent self-interest. Ask yourself this question, if you want to measure it in yourself, not what action is justified, but what action will lead me to do what is to my intelligent self-interest. The ability to see through the emotional fabric is the first key of excellence and leadership.

The second key is that we must make decisions. Research has proven that there are two kinds of people in the world. There are people who say, "If I don't try, there is no way I can fail." Failure is to be avoided at all costs. But there is another group who say, "If I don't try there is no way I can succeed. If I try I have a chance for both success or failure."

It is like the fellow in Pecos, Texas. He walked into the smithy shop where the smithy had his foot going on the forge, pumping it white hot. The smithy picked up a horseshoe with the tines, shook the coals off and tossed it to the old sod buster. He reached up and grabbed it then quickly tossed it down. The Smithy said, without missing a pump, "Hot, ain't it?" The sod buster said, "No, just don't take me long to look at a horseshoe." Decision making, the ability to make a decision, to jump in and say, "I'm going to give it a go," is certainly part of excellence and leadership.

The third key is we must learn to be patient and tolerant. Have an affinity for and love of the uniqueness of each person's contribution. This is the root system that holds people together and yet gives them their own identity in the labyrinth of the underpinning of life. How patient must you be? I think Job had something to say about that. 'The patience you must exhibit is that which transcends all frustrations."

You must be patient in managing the skills of others. Never set standards for others that you set for yourself. Set a standard for others that's based on their capabilities, not yours. You see, if you are to teach and transfer, to give to others the benefit of what you've learned, you must give it willingly, completely, without any expectation of a refund of value. If you do this, you will be a true coach and sponsor.

It's like the parents, Cy and Mary, at the dinner table. Mary says to Cy, "How come you tell Junior 20 times how to hold his fork?" Cy says, "Because 19 isn't enough."

In my junior year in high school, my father was not patient. Picture this. It's Saturday evening and I have a date with a young lady and all I have left to get is $5.00 and the family car from my father. You can imagine how many times I heard, "Boy it's sure different than when I courted your Mom! A buck and a half took us both to the movie, we each had a cheese sandwich and a Coke on the way to the movie . . . and another thing, we used to walk 8 1/2 miles from the farm into Yukon, Oklahoma and back! What do you think of that? I had nothing to do with coming along in 1935. I'm there late for a date needing two things, five bucks and wheels! Finally, in my senior year, my father got very brilliant. Maybe he always had it and I just discovered it! He finally set standards for me in terms I could understand. Can Allan operate the car safely? Does he have a driver's license? Can Allan spend within the $5 budget? Can he show enough personal discipline to come home at a reasonable hour and not wake his mother and me or the neighbors next door or the whole community at 3 a.m. driving across their lawns singing "When the Saints Come Marching In?" Can Allan show the discipline and tolerance?

And Key number four, as managers, you must recognize the differences in people. I maintain that there are three general types of employees. The first group I will speak about is a group I call the Hermans and the Marthas.

You recognize them by what they do, not what they look like. You soon learn to know what they look like by what they do. Here are their traits. Number one, and clearly the most beneficial is that they set a standard of performance higher than you, their boss, would set for them. You find you never have to talk to them about performance. They are already one step ahead of you. They may even come early to get a jump on the day, and they do it without making you, the supervisor, feel guilty. The standard they work toward is understood and clear . . . and if they don't understand, they are secure enough to ask.

You ever notice how the Hermans and the Marthas are very gentle with those people who let them down? They say, "It was my responsibility to check with you." They also are loyal to a fault. They don't want to transfer or move. They won't even think about a job offer from another firm. They tend to respect authority. If you call a meeting at 3 a.m. on Sunday morning, they'll ask which door they should come in. That's the Hermans and the Marthas.

Another thing I notice about them is that they never talk long at coffee breaks and certainly not about gossip. The minute you start to talk about somebody who isn't there they demonstrate excellence by getting up and leaving quietly. They don't want to be in an arena in which they may contribute to something that does not build.

The Hermans and the Marthas are delights to manage. You seldom have to tell them anything; you only present the situation and they see things they could do. They generally represent 15-20% of your employees.

The other end of the scale is a group I call the Red Ants or "Ormiga Kojas." A Red Ant has the goal each day to have as much work to do at the end of eight hours of pay as there was in the beginning, or, the "Red Ant Emeritus" is to have more work to do at the end of eight hours of pay as there was at the beginning. In order to accomplish this they will even undo their own work or others.

They are a bane on corporate life. They're there to tear up and confuse and serve selfish interests. They're against everything you're for. They argue on every issue; they'll take the devil's advocate position, not to add clarity to thinking but to add confusion and take away focus. They tend to not relate at all to the Hermans and the Marthas. They stay away from and are not comfortable with the Hermans and the Marthas. They create havoc in the company. The Red Ants are 10 to 15% of the work force.

When Red Ants get into the computer world, you've really got problems. A computer can be a very excellent decision-making tool, but it is also a device that can do more wrong in less time than anything ever designed. In fact, it can bring you bad information quick enough for you to take action on it. You're able, therefore, to go in the wrong direction with a greater degree of certainty! However, it also can do more correctly and bring you good data on which to base a sound decision.

Example, did you ever try to get out of the Book of the Month Club? I ordered a book and it came in the cardboard package with the 80 columnar, 12-line card inside the envelope. I took it out and the amount due was $6.40. I sent it away and started reading the book. Two weeks later I got a notice that said my account was now overdue and to please remit promptly. Well, I looked at the amount due below and it was $00.00, so I pitched it. Two weeks later I got a third notice. It said "do not disregard."

I ripped it open promptly and it read, "Your account is now seriously overdue. Please send your check in the enclosed envelope. Or else..." I looked at the amount again and it was 00.00, so I pitched it. Two weeks later I got a letter that read, "Congratulations, your account has now been turned over for collection. Fifty-five percent interest has been added to the amount due below."

Now I wasn't number one in my mathematics class, but I remember one clear fact. That is, anything times zero is zero. I started to pitch it when I realized that I wasn't talking to a human being, I was talking to a computer. So I sat down and wrote to the computer something it could understand. It was a check for 00.00 and I sent it back in the postage paid envelope. I received a letter saying thanks for my late payment, (late being underlined). It said to please remit the 80 columnar, 12-line card to remove my name from the delinquent account list of the Retail Credit Bureau of America. Terrific, zero balance and lousy credit. It caught me on a bad day I guess and it had the three Beatitudes of Computerdom printed on it: Do not fold, spindle or mutilate. Well, I just couldn't pass it up. You know what I did? I crushed it into a small ball, stapled it on the four corners, spindled it six times across the face. Then I sent it back. I got a hand-written personal note from the manager of data processing. It said, "Please, don't ever do that again." So that Red Ant that creates problems should be gotten rid of.

The third group is called the Vanillas. They're the ones who go into a Baskin-Robbins store that has 92 flavors and ask for vanilla. If they want to stretch quantum leaps into the future they say, "I'll have french vanilla with marshmallow topping." They're a tint base. They're that which is waiting for the color of the day.

I'm certain that when I go home at the end of this week on the front of our fridge door will be something. By the way, the maximum accolade for anything that comes into our home is to go on the front of the fridge door with the magnets. We've got so many magnets on the front of our fridge door that a steel can of pineapple juice from Dole came from the back of that fridge to the door the other day. Anyway, on our fridge door is a BEMAR List — Backlog Of Essential Maintenance and Repair. Some know it as the 'Honey Do' list.

There will be some things there that I have to paint on Saturday. I'll go down to the paint store and talk with the paint expert. We'll pick a color and put it into the can of tint base with the appropriate measurements for color and tint.

That is the employee that occupies 60-80% of your time. They are the ones who have no color. They believe that if they show up and are clean, scrubbed, and dressed, they have done all that they are supposed to do. They come to work and say, "I'm here, now what are you going to do with me?" You say, "Well, why don't you just continue doing what you did yesterday?" They say, "Well, could you go over that again? I've sort of put it out of my mind."

You would evaluate them as people who do not have an interest in your business. I suggest that you look at them in a different way, as raw material. Raw material is something that needs to be upgraded, to be given a bigger horizon. Someone you stretch so that they have a chance to grow with the opportunity that you create. Vanillas are something to behold because they tend to put out of their mind those things that they've done well in the past. They are afraid to make a mistake. Vanillas go home and the problem is in the pillows. They put their heads on the pillow and all the color acquired during the day drains off into the pillow. They have to get another tint the next day.

Now, in managing these three, and here's where we get to the decision process, we get to do something that's to your intelligent self-interest. When you end your patience and tolerance you manage each differently. The Hermans and the Marthas, for example, you manage as peers. You share with them: Here's what we're after, what do you think you might contribute? When do you think it can be done? They tend to respond with a realistic answer.

How do you deal with the Vanillas? The Vanillas need constant positive direction every day. They are 60-80% of the people you run into. They need the reinforcement of what is to be done next so you must put the emphasis on the expectation. The Vanillas tend to respond to that. They tend to only then say "no" when they don't understand. They'll want you to go over it a little bit more in detail. Whenever a Vanilla asks for detail, take a book and open it up and write down exactly the things that you want him to do. Then give him that sheet of paper. Give him the next step to do.

The Red Ant is quite different. We must call upon a skill that is not born within each of us. Here is the way to handle a Red Ant. There are three things you do. Number one, you fire with honor. Number two, isolate them. Give them work in the proverbial Siberia so that nothing they do is dependent on anyone else or no one is waiting for the output of their labor. Isolate them, get them totally out of the system and let them do their thing. Third, load them up. Give them more work than many people could do in a reasonable amount of time and expect them to do it.

The first one, firing with honor, is the true art of management. There are three phrases that I would like you to commit to memory. Firing with honor must possess all three of these ideas expressed in these phrases. First, "I choose to no longer purchase the skills you bring to work." Second, "Inside you is a heck of a worker that on occasion has come out, but has not come out often enough or stayed out long enough for me to continue to add you to overhead." Third, "I share a part of the responsibility — not enough to keep you, but enough to tell you that I did not manage you correctly."

You see, firing with honor says that they must leave with some shred of true self-esteem and self-regard. Because you see, inside every Red Ant is a Herman or a Martha who is just uncomfortable at coming out. You are the hard-nosed manager, but you will be the respected manager because they will come back and thank you for demanding more from them than anyone they had ever worked for.

The ability to deal with these three different types says that I must not have just one skill. Excellence is dealing with that which I find. It's dealing with that hot horseshoe. It is the ability then to make a decision to do what's to my intelligent self-interest, to be patient and tolerant.

The last demand of excellence is that we must dismiss personal grudges promptly. We cannot let that anger, that vanity, hang on and be a sea anchor to our forward progress. We must look to the future and dismiss personal grudges immediately. They keep you from moving forward and clearing the air.

Tact is that invaluable ingredient. Tact, by definition, is the oil that smooths out the bearings. It's the lubricant that eases the friction that's going to occur any time you put people together. I know someone's gone too far when I hear him say, "Well, I can tell you one thing or, to be perfectly frank..." Well, don't be. Be tactful. The ability to apply your knowledge and skill to the next moment is the first step in that quantum movement to the great expectation that you have of yourself.

I close with a story. It's the story of a wise old man. He was so wise that he astounded everyone in the community. In that crowd was a Red Ant who belittled and talked down to the old man. He thought the old man was an idiot and publicly said so.

He thought, "I must devise a scheme to disgrace the old man in front of his peers. I'll catch a bird from the field and I'll gather everyone into the town square. I'll hold the bird in my hand and I will ask the old man, "If you are wise, tell me is the bird alive or is it dead?" No matter how he answers I will cause the other to happen and therefore make him be thought of as a fool.

So the day came, and the legions came and sat upon the hillside. The old man was there in his robes. The young man had a bird in his hands and said to him, "Old man, be ye so wise, tell me is this bird alive or is it dead?" The old man said, with the wisdom of his ages, "It is in your hands my son. It is in your hands." And so it is with your pursuit, your challenge and your acceptance of excellence. It is in your hands!

20

LEADERSHIP THROUGH COACHING

Don Thoren
5410 Lakeshore Dr. #A
Tempe, AZ 85283
602/838-7406

When my client/friend, Dan Duval, was elected President of a billion dollar Ohio corporation, he was already the product of many years of coaching by other people. As he was preparing to travel to the subsidiaries and introduce his programs, I "coached" him to use the following joke as an "ice-breaker" for those presentations. The joke describes the new company president whose predecessor said, "My coaching advice to you is contained in this contingency plan consisting of these three envelopes labeled one, two, and three. The first time you have a problem you don't know how to solve, open envelope number one for it contains a guaranteed solution. Save envelope two as long as you can before using it and save envelope three for as many years as possible." The new president was appreciative of this "coaching" help and stored the envelopes safely in his desk drawer. A few months later, he had a problem he had tried two or three ways to solve unsuccessfully. He reached in the drawer for envelope number one, opened it and the advice was: "Regardless of what the problem is, blame it on me and that will give you additional time to seek a solution."

A couple of years later, he found a need to go back to the drawer for envelope number two and it said, "Reorganize, it will buy you at least another six months!" So he reorganized and found that the promise of letter two was also true. The reorganization not only bought him some time, but some of it actually resulted in some improvement!

A few years later he found himself confronted by a problem which seemed to defy solution, and as much as he hated to use it up, he reached for envelope three. With optimistic expectation he read the solution but was shocked by its message: "It is now your turn to prepare three envelopes for your successor!" By telling the joke, Dan got the desired laugh and by making himself the object of the joke, he gained added rapport with some of his more nervous audiences.

Leadership through coaching, as I would like to discuss it in this chapter, is never delivered by letter and always arrives in time to prevent failure. I believe that the foundation for coaching in business is a lot like the key coaching element in athletics. Who are your competitors and what kind of a game plan does it take to win in this league? That game plan might be a business project, a whole new corporate change, or for most managers, simply their best attempts to make some marginal improvements in the performance of some not so glamorous job responsibilities. Your set of players could be a management staff, a group of sales people, service people, manufacturing people, etc. I believe that excellence in leadership through coaching is revealed when you are able to get above average results out of average people!

In athletics, it's one thing to have a winning game plan, quite another thing to find or develop the players who can execute that optimum plan. Organizational coaching also requires a constant sacrifice of the optimal plan and the constant development of people to achieve the next best results. Leadership through coaching is not necessarily leadership by example. One of the things that most frustrates me is hearing a manager proudly state, "I never ask my people to do anything that I'm not able to do myself," thinking that this makes him a pinnacle of virtue. But the real impact of that philosophy is to forever handicap the organization's potential with the limitations of its leadership. Even in professional athletics the best coaches were seldom the best players. Therefore, leadership through coaching is having a vision of what could be and developing others to their fullest potential in the pursuit of that vision.

Here's a graphic example of what I mean by having and sharing a vision. On one of my many airplane flights I had just gotten settled down to do some paper work when my seatmate introduced himself. It became evident very quickly that this was going to be a talking ride! Perhaps you have had that same experience yourself. My seatmate had a very engaging personality so I put my materials away and decided I might just as well enjoy the conversation. He turned out to be an executive recruiter for a very prestigious executive search firm in New York City. Since the management of change is a constant theme in all of my management and sales seminars, I felt that this person would certainly have to be an effective change agent and I could learn some new ideas from him. His firm specialized in finding candidates for policy making executive positions with the world's largest corporations where the salaries are measured in the hundreds of thousands. Now, that really got my attention as a salary like that would give me a chance to get out of speaking, writing, and training, and try doing real work for a change! My seatmate enthusiastically volunteered lots of information about how he evaluated candidates and how he sought to provide a good "fit" between the person and the job.

All of this activity however, I knew had to be reduced to the bottom-line of getting somebody to change jobs — the change agent role. I confessed an awareness for how difficult it must be for the recruiter to get others to change jobs when they have already achieved the monetary and status success necessary to be considered as a candidate for one of these jobs. I could picture the difficulty of trying to get someone to leave a trusted team for a group of strangers, leave one geographic climate for another, leave one industry for another, etc. I asked my seatmate the bottom-line question, "What is the most critical factor contributing to a person's willingness to change jobs?" He indicated to me that actually it was rather simple. He said, "Don, they change jobs because they are so unhappy." Well, that made sense to me as we all read alot about executive stress and unhappiness. Another thought occurred to me and I had one final question, "Answer me this. How do you know when they are so unhappy?" He responded, "That's just the point, Don. They may not be — not at least until I start talking to them and creating a new vision for their future!" Anyone who has ever been called by a "head hunter" understands the truth of that statement. But most leaders fail to recognize how to use the same principle for "coaching" better results out of their own people.

There are two great sources of motivational coaching visions: Unrealized opportunities and unresolved problems. The book, *In Search of Excellence*, advocates "management by walking around," and some of my clients asked me for suggested topics of discussions while they were "walking around." I suggested a "typhoid Mary" kind of approach — constantly spreading the "germs" of unrealized opportunities and unresolved problems. Keep talking, keep painting the vision of a new reality that *could* be.

One of my own sources for learning that lesson was my "fatherhood" consultant, Bill McGrane III. Bill is about five years older than my own son and since I admired Bill so much, I asked him what were some of the most helpful things his father had done for him. He described how his own father had made a habit of driving him to high school on every possible occasion just to be with him and talk with him. Young Bill admitted that his own lack of interest in a topic never deterred his dad from continuing to enthusiastically hammer away at the principles for success and happiness.

When my son, Jeff, at age twenty-two, agreed to join the family for a one-year sabbatical to Hawaii I practiced Bill McGrane's advice. As Jeff and I walked the beach, I talked! Sure I also asked questions and tried to be a good listener, but I never let his listening mood deter me from enthusiastically describing all of the opportunities available to him and the success principles for capturing them.

In more "text book" terms, we say to establish the standard or responsibilities for each employee. In other words, be as specific as possible in telling people what you expect in the way of the performance and the results. I would add this additional thought from my own life experience — make those standards as measurable and obvious as possible so that the person has an optimum opportunity to self-manage his own learning and performance. For example, when my daughter, Kate was ready to learn snow skiing this "professional communicator" decided to teach her himself. Kate learned to balance herself going straight down the "bunny" hill very quickly and I decided to teach her how to make turns as preparation for steeper slopes. After 30 minutes of my best "coaching" on how to make turns I was failing miserably and called in a ski instructor. Sizing up the situation, her first advice was for me to go ski for an hour! When I returned Kate was making beautiful turns and I asked her what the instructor had said that I had failed to say. Kate explained she had told her mostly the same things however, in addition, she had taken all four ski poles and placed them in the snow at twenty yard intervals down the slope. She told Kate that if she could make the turns to get between each of the poles on her way down then she would have the necessary skills to try steeper slopes. Why hadn't I thought of that! The ski instructor provided a clearly understood performance standard, placed performance responsibility squarely on Kate, and then let Kate use her as necessary to achieve her own success. Can you make the expectations you have for those responding to your leadership through coaching more specific and self-manageable?

Step two of the fundamentals is to simply observe the

employee's performance and compare it to the standards. Let me make a big distinction here. I'm not just talking about reviewing the results, I'm talking about observing the performance. When my friend, James Watt, was Secretary of the Interior, he automatically practiced management by walking around long before it became fashionable. One of the great assets James brought to his position was a broad scope of knowledge gained through two decades of working with Congressional Committees, The U.S. Chamber of Commerce, serving a presidential appointment to the Federal Power Commission and other top jobs at the Department of Interior. James loved to drop in on employees at various levels of the organization to have them simply describe to him the approaches they were using to achieve their results. He never used these occasions for criticism but rather to provide encouragement, additional sources of information and his own suggestions. These he could provide because of his own in-depth knowledge.

A lot of leaders are handicapped today because they simply are not well schooled in the technology they are trying to manage. I helped spread that philosophy in the early days of my experience with General Electric when we believed that a good manager could manage any business regardless of product knowledge. In my later motivational work I believed that a good salesman could move the product without detailed product knowledge. I have changed my mind! The leaders who today cover up a lack of knowledge by insisting that they are too busy managing the larger policy initiatives are copping out. You would not stand for it in the way your own government representatives perform so why would your subordinates accept it from you?

Learning the work so you can be a helpful observer of the performance is critical to leadership through coaching. Could you imagine a professional football coach, say Tom Landry of the Dallas Cowboys, practicing his team all week and then not going to watch the game? It would be unheard of, you say? Thousands of sales managers conduct sales meetings on Monday morning but then never go into the field during the week to observe the sales people "playing the game." And I'm only talking about observing, not demonstrating or trying to save the sale for them. The observation must be complete just as a medical diagnosis must be complete before the treatment plan can change the final outcome.

The third fundamental of coaching is to provide feedback. Feedback on the plus or minus consequences of the performance you observe as it relates to the employee achieving the established standards. The athletic coach observes the players performance to reinforce what is being done correctly and to correct what is being done incorrectly. It's the same process in organizations. Reinforcing what was done properly leads to conscious competence and improves the probability the desired performance will be repeated in the future. Correcting the performance begins with showing it's adverse consequences on the accomplishment of the end result.

Keep corrections objective and do not sugar coat them. Review the elements of the performance observed in the sequence they happened and reinforce or correct in the same sequence. This advice is contrary to that offered in many management programs which suggest that any criticism should be "sandwiched" between two compliments. The theory of the "sandwich" technique is that the critique will then be easier to swallow! It is a wonderful analogy but a disastrous practice. A practice, which as described by my friend Art Secord, causes the first compliment to put a big smile on their face so that when you kick their teeth in with the critique, you won't cut their lips! In other words, it's dishonest and manipulative. If you use that technique you will find that your compliments are meaningless as they become viewed as a set-up for a kick in the teeth.

People don't mind constructively critical feedback that helps them to eliminate mistakes or to achieve higher performance in their job responsibilities. You don't mind do you? Neither will they. After all, we all received a school report card every six weeks for twelve to eighteen years! We are conditioned to receiving feedback for self-management purposes.

When you describe an employee's performance and relate its impact on the results to be achieved, you are creating opportunities for employee self-management. Life showed me a personal application of that principle a few years ago when I was on my way to give a speech in Denver. First of all, our airport in Phoenix has been perpetually under construction since 1903! Naturally, on the morning that I am running late to catch my flight, the parking lots are being resurfaced and I can't find a place to park my car. In my frustration, I find what appears to be safe spot to park and jump out to dash to the terminal. A workman quickly calls to me, "Hey, buddy—you gotta move that car or it will be towed away." I am now embarrassed when I think back on how rudely I treated that workman. I gave him a piece of my mind about how poorly the construction was marked, about what a terribly important person I was, and about how my car was going to stay where it was until I got back from Denver that evening. Needless to say, I was overpowering and he was overwhelmed. As I turned to dash away, he timidly lamented, "Well, OK, but they will tow it away." His message to me contained eight words. These eight words, weakly spoken, none the less described a vivid picture of the consequences of my actions. My objective had been to use my car to get to *and* from the airport. I am now thankful that the workman overlooked my rudeness and through a description of consequences gave me a self-management choice to meet my own objective—I moved the car! I caught my flight to Denver and gave my speech to the personnel management members of the Rocky Mountain Employers Council. And yes, I used the example of what the airport workman had taught me about the gift you give others when you help them understand the consequences of their actions!

For any of you who may feel that you simply don't have time to "coach" those who support you, let me suggest that coaching is not an "add-on" activity. It is an integral part of delegating work and assuring completion. Whether we think of it as coaching or not, all leaders have more projects to accomplish than they have personal time to complete them.

Telling others specifically what you want done, observing at least a part of how they do it, and providing feedback on their performance is the best way I know to save time. Good coaching!